A Princess's Pilgrimage

Courtesy: British Library

Siobhan Lambert-Hurley's publications have brought to light the story of a remarkable family of Muslim women, successive rulers of one of the British colonial princely states, who defy many conventional stereotypes. This volume reprints the account of an 1863-64 pilgrimage to Mecca undertaken by the formidable Nawab Sikandar Begum. As Lambert-Hurley argues in an illuminating introduction, the Nawab used the occasion in part to define her own colonially-inflected vision of leadership and good governance against the Ottoman example of rule she encountered in Arabia first hand. Readers interested in a very wide range of subjects, including Indian history, Muslim women, and Islam in the colonial period, will welcome this book.

Barbara D. Metcalf
Alice Freeman Palmer Professor of History
University of Michigan

Lambert-Hurley's thoughtful and carefully plotted introduction to Sikandar Begum's text allows us to appreciate the role of the Hajj in announcing the arrival of a gendered Muslim self, and in enunciating the limits and possibilities of travel for an elite Muslim woman in the colonial world. This is a must-read for students of gender, imperial, post/colonial and Middle Eastern histories.

Antoinette Burton
Professor and Chair, Department of History
University of Illinois

A Princess's Pilgrimage

Nawab Sikandar Begum's *A Pilgrimage to Mecca*

Edited, Introduced and with an Afterword by
SIOBHAN LAMBERT-HURLEY

A Princess's Pilgrimage
is published outside South Asia and the US by

Kube Publishing
Markfield Conference Centre
Ratby Lane, Markfield
Leics LE67 9SY, England

Kube Publishing have decided to adhere to the original Arabic translation in this book. This does not in some cases conform to our house style.

British Library Cataloguing in Publication Data

Begum, Nawab Sikandar
A pilgrimage to Mecca
1. Begum, Nawab Sikandar – Travel – Saudi Arabia
2. Muslim pilgrims and pilgrimages – Saudi Arabia – Mecca
3. Saudi Arabia – Description and travel
I. Title
297.3'52'092

ISBN: 9781847740014 PB

Cover design: Nasir Cadir

CONTENTS

PREFACE AND ACKNOWLEDGEMENTS

PILGRIMAGE in Islam may be distinguished from the practice in other religious traditions by its obligatory nature. In order to fulfil the requirements of the Islamic faith as elucidated in the Qur'an and traditions, every Muslim, male and female, must make a scripted visit to the Ka'aba in Mecca during the assigned month of Dill-Hijja at least once in their lifetime, if they can afford it. The limits on this tenet have meant that most Muslims throughout history have not fulfilled this obligation, though numbers have increased substantially in the modern age. Pilgrim sex ratios are not available, but it is clear that women have made up a fair percentage of those going on hajj from the earliest days of Islam, not only from contemporary reports, but also from their own accounts of the journey.[1] This book focuses on one woman's account of hajj, making it

[1] The rudiments of the preface to this point are borrowed from my entry on pilgrimage in Islam for the *Encyclopedia of Sex and Gender* (Macmillan Reference USA, forthcoming).

available to a contemporary audience after it was first published in 1870, but has been out of print for over a hundred years. Written by an Indian Muslim princess, this text, *A Pilgrimage to Mecca*, offers a gendered view of the hajj in its traditional form, before advances in transportation and communication altered the experience of Islamic pilgrimage so dramatically in the twentieth century. Nawab Sikandar Begum, the author, is an engaging narrator who provides a critical and often surprising account of her hajj experience that encourages the reader—whether scholar, student or enthusiast—to rethink established understandings relating to travel writing, colonialism and world history.

These points are developed in the first section of this book in an introduction intended to situate and interpret Nawab Sikandar Begum's hajj narrative within its appropriate historical and literary context. It is an extended version of a paper published under the title 'A Princess's Pilgrimage: Nawab Sikandar Begum's Account of Hajj' in Tim Youngs (ed.), *Travel in the Nineteenth Century: Filling in the Blank Spaces* (London: Anthem, 2006: pp. 107–27). I extend my thanks to the editor of this volume, also my colleague at Nottingham Trent University, for encouraging me to write on this topic in the first place and helping me to focus my ideas in the early stages. Earlier versions of this paper were also presented at seminars at the Nehru Memorial Museum and Library, New Delhi, 14 February 2006; the Royal Asiatic Society, London, 9 March 2006; and

Boston University, 27 April 2006. I am indebted to the organisers and participants on those occasions for raising important issues that I have tried to incorporate into this revised version. Thanks also to Patrick Mark, my collaborator on another travel-related project, for many animated discussions on the subject of Muslim travellers, as well as Michael Fisher, Barbara Metcalf, Antoinette Burton and Ashlee Cunsolo for their thoughtful comments on an earlier draft.

In the next section of this book, Nawab Sikandar Begum's narrative is reproduced in its entirety from Mrs E.L. Willoughby-Osborne's original English translation with the original title page, dedication and preface. The two appendices—a 'sketch' of Bhopal history and a 'descriptive list of the holy places of Arabia'—are omitted on the basis that their contextual function is provided by my introduction in which their content is also summarised. Instead, the translation is followed here by an afterword that provides a brief survey of travel writing written by Muslim women *after* Sikandar Begum about their journeys out of South Asia. The hope is that this short essay—an earlier version of which is to be published in Shobhana Bhattacharji (ed.), *Travel Writing in India* (Delhi: Sahitya Akademi, forthcoming)—will, along with the bibliography that follows, direct the reader captured by Sikandar's narrative to related secondary and primary material, thus making this small book a comprehensive resource on travel writing by South Asian Muslim women. For encouraging me to pursue this project in this way and directing me expertly through the publication process, I owe a huge debt of gratitude to Ritu Menon and her staff at Women Unlimited in Delhi. I also acknowledge the essential funding provided by the British Academy and HEFCE's Promising Researcher Scheme to allow me to complete the necessary fieldwork in South Asia in the winter of 2005-6. During that time, this work benefited from so many lively conversations with wonderful friends in Delhi, not all of whom I can mention here. As always, my husband, Josh, deserves a medal for his patience throughout the research and writing process. But I know he will understand if I dedicate this book instead to the memory of our little boy.

Allah hi deta hai, Allah hi leta hai

Siobhan Lambert-Hurley
Nottingham
December 2006

AN INTRODUCTION TO NAWAB SIKANDAR BEGUM'S ACCOUNT OF HAJJ

Siobhan Lambert-Hurley

WOMEN TRAVELLERS, MUSLIM TRAVELLERS

BETWEEN July and October 2004, the National Portrait Gallery in London featured a special exhibition entitled 'Off the Beaten Track: Three Centuries of Women Travellers'. It highlighted the journeys of predominantly British women as they travelled to other parts of the globe, including the Americas, Africa and Asia, between the 1660s and the 1960s. Only in the final section of the exhibition, in a small corner to itself, did it recognise women travelling in other directions, specifically 'a selection of the world's women who made Britain their destination'.[1] Of these twelve, four hailed from the Indian subcontinent, while just two were Muslims: Princess Dur-i-Shahvar of Berar, daughter of the last Turkish Caliph and daughter-in-law of the last ruling

[1] 'Off the Beaten Track: Three Centuries of Women Travellers,' National Portrait Gallery, 7 July–31 October 2004. See also Dea Birkett, *Off the Beaten Track: Three Centuries of Women Travellers* (London: National Portrait Gallery, 2004).

Nizam of Hyderabad, and Begum Zubeida Habib Rahimtoola, wife of the first High Commissioner for Pakistan in the United Kingdom. That these women were included at all is certainly to be commended for its recognition of South Asian and Muslim women's participation in the culture of travel, yet their few numbers and bounded location suggest the marginalisation of their experiences, even as their stories provide unique insight into the places they visited, the people they met, and the changes they underwent as individuals as part of the journey. As one elderly gentleman commented rather aptly as he rounded the corner to face these women's portraits, 'Well, this is quite a different kettle of fish.'

Over the past two decades, some scholarly writers have sought to capture the experiences of 'this kettle of fish' as part of the project of historicising Britain's multiculturalism and deconstructing colonial encounters. A pioneering effort in this direction was Rozina Visram's *Ayahs, Lascars and Princes* in which she documented the substantial numbers of Indians, many of whom were Muslim and some of whom were female, who resided in Britain in the capacity of servants, sailors and labourers from the early eighteenth century.[2] The explicitly gendered nature of these 'cultures of travel' was

[2] Rozina Visram, *Ayahs, Lascars and Princes* (London: Pluto Press, 1986). Also see Rozina Visram, *Asians in Britain: 400 Years of History* (London: Pluto Press, 2002).

subsequently drawn out by Inderpal Grewal and Antoinette Burton through a focus on Indian women that sojourned 'at the heart of the empire' in the high Victorian period, the most well-known being Pandita Ramabai (1858-1922) and Cornelia Sorabji (1866-1954)—the latter even being pictured in the NPG exhibition.[3] It is only very recently, however, that Michael Fisher has explored in any depth the way in which Indian women travelled to Britain from the earliest years of contact between Britain and the subcontinent, not only as the wives and daughters of Indians and Britons, but also as servants, slaves and independent noblewomen in a 'counterflow to colonialism'. One prominent example of a Muslim woman who fulfilled this function was the Queen Mother of Awadh, who, as a veiled woman accompanied by a large coterie of exotically dressed attendants, attracted the curiosity of the British press—though not always in a sympathetic fashion—

[3] Inderpal Grewal, *Home and Harem: Nation, Gender, Empire, and the Cultures of Travel* (London: Leicester University Press, 1996); and Antoinette Burton, *At the Heart of the Empire: Indians and the Colonial Encounter in Late-Victorian Britain* (New Delhi: Munshiram Manoharlal, 1998). Also see my own work on the journeys of Sultan Jahan Begum of Bhopal to Britain in the early twentieth century in Siobhan Lambert-Hurley, 'Out of India: The Journeys of the Begam of Bhopal, 1901-1930,' *Women's Studies' International Forum*, 21:3 (June, 1998), pp. 263-76; reprinted in Tony Ballantyne, and Antoinette Burton (eds.), *Bodies in Contact: Rethinking Colonial Encounters in World History* (Durham: Duke University Press, 2005), pp. 293-309.

when she visited the imperial capital in 1856-7 to protest the annexation of her son's kingdom.[4] Even less celebrated were the many cases of bonded servants, a fair percentage of whom—certainly larger than their share of the population as a whole—appear from Fisher's evidence to have been Muslim women.[5]

What this latter example suggests is that South Asian Muslims, whether male or female, were enabled by established patterns of movement within the Islamic world to go abroad in larger numbers and with greater ease than many of their fellow Indians. The assumption may be that they took motivation from a religious doctrine that prescribes travel for the purpose of hajj (pilgrimage), hijra (emigration) and *rihla* (learning and other purposes), among others, and that, if inspired by one of these forms of ritual movement, they would have been drawn closer to their faith and fellow Muslims through the experience.[6] Yet, as Dale F. Eickelman and James Piscatori have argued, this phenomenon of the 'Muslim traveller' is actually far more complex if one accepts that their journeys, like those of other travellers, are as much about a 'journey of the mind', an 'inventive journey', as 'temporal movement'. Not only is the point of departure—'home'—reimagined through the process

4 Michael H. Fisher, *Counterflows to Colonialism: Indian Travellers and Settlers in Britain 1600-1857* (Delhi: Permanent Black, 2004), pp. 411-22.

5 Fisher, *Counterflows*, pp. 222-4.

6 See, for instance, Grewal, *Home and Harem*, p. 140.

of travel, but so, too, are notions of 'self' and 'other'—even if that 'other' is Muslim. To be sure, one of the great ironies to emerge from Eickelman and Piscatori's edited collection is the way in which Muslims travelling to other parts of the Islamic world expected to be enveloped by a sense of Muslim solidarity—the 'spiritual unity of the *umma*'—yet, as often, found their 'consciousness of locality and difference' heightened.[7]

This introduction aims to explore some of these possibilities relating to women and Muslim travellers by analysing the hajj narrative of one exemplary woman, Sikandar Begum (1816-68). She ruled the Muslim princely state of Bhopal in central India, first as regent from 1844 until 1860, then as full-fledged nawab from 1860 to 1868. Her account of 'a pilgrimage to Mecca', undertaken in 1863-4, was first published in 1870 after being translated into English from the original Urdu manuscript by the wife of a British colonial officer, Mrs Emma Laura Willoughby-Osborne (1835-1905). In her 'translator's preface', she noted that she had embarked on this task on the basis that an account of this nature by a 'Mahomedan Princess' would surely be of interest to the general reader. She listed four reasons as justification: first, because no 'work' written by an 'Eastern lady' had, to her knowledge, ever been

[7] Dale F. Eickelman, and James Piscatori (eds.), *Muslim Travellers: Pilgrimage, Migration, and the Religious Imagination* (London: Routledge, 1990), pp. xii-xv.

published; second, because very few European travellers had visited Mecca; third, because, in her words, 'the opportunity of viewing things from an Oriental point of view is a novel one'; and, fourth, because the author had already earned herself a reputation in India and England for the 'sagacity, shrewdness and enlightenment' of her administration, as well as her loyalty to the British government during the recent 'Sepoy War'.[8] Though her assumptions about Indian women's literary output may not have been entirely accurate, most of these reasons do, in some way, still have resonance well over a hundred years later and, thus, offer at least partial explanation as to why this particular text warrants detailed attention.

In analysing this narrative, this introduction will highlight three main themes. First, it will examine the text's location within an Islamic tradition of travel writing as negotiated within a colonial context. Issues of motivation, audience, structure and style will be addressed, as well as the possible reasoning behind the book's published form. It will then seek to identify ways in which notions of the self were depicted in this narrative, questioning whether Sikandar's main aim was to chart a personal journey of faith, as one may expect, or craft an identity more closely related to political concerns. In the third section, it will turn to investigating

[8] E.L. Willoughby-Osborne, 'Translator's Preface' in The Nawab Sikandar Begum of Bhopal, *A Pilgrimage to Mecca*, tr. Mrs Willoughby-Osborne (London: Wm H. Allen & Co., 1870).

the Begum's perception of Arabia—the 'other'—as an alternative construction of 'the Orient'. Her travelogue will, thus, be treated as a form of ethnography in which her perspectives on gender roles, sanitation and religious practice can be revealed. A final section will then offer some concluding thoughts on what can be gained in terms of our understanding of travel and travel writing from looking at the hajj narrative of an Indian Muslim woman. Together, this analysis will provide insight into a spiritual journey that, while influenced by the colonial milieu, remained distinct from any European experience of travel. Before tackling these various issues, however, some explication needs to be provided of Mrs Willoughby-Osborne's final point in order to locate the author, her journey and her text within its appropriate historical context.

Bhopal, Paramountcy and the Indian Pilgrimage

Bhopal, the state ruled by Sikandar in the mid-nineteenth century, was one of nearly six hundred principalities—encompassing two-fifths of the area and one-third of the population of the British Indian Empire—that retained nominal independence in the colonial period. This imperial system, known as 'subsidiary alliance' or 'paramountcy', was established as a result of a series of 'treaties of friendship and cooperation' that were negotiated between regional Indian states and the East India Company in the late eighteenth and early nineteenth centuries, 1818 in the case of Bhopal. According to these agreements, 'princely' or 'native' states, as they came to be known, retained their own rulers, systems of law and even rudimentary military forces, but sacrificed control of their foreign affairs to the British overlord and accepted the appointment of a resident British adviser. In Bhopal, this figure was the political agent who was based at the British cantonment at Sehore approximately twenty-five miles from the state capital. Significantly, it was this post that Mrs Willoughby-Osborne's husband, Lieutenant Colonel (later Colonel) John William Willoughby-Osborne (1833-1881), filled at various points between 1863 and 1881 in alternation with that of resident in neighbouring Gwalior.[9]

It is worth noting that, in the period before 1857, these formal treaties between the Company and the 'native princes' were often abrogated—a key example already mentioned being that of Awadh in 1856—on the basis of administrative inefficiency or the lack of a natural male heir. The latter were in short supply in Bhopal throughout the nineteenth century for the simple reason that no male children were born into the family for four generations. Yet Sikandar's mother, Qudsia (1801-1881), was able to convince the British overlord that she be allowed to rule as regent until her daughter came of age and married—at which time her son-in-law would restore male succession—after the accidental

[9] C.E. Luard, *Bhopal State Gazetteer*, vol. III (Calcutta: Superintendent Government Printing India, 1908), p. 129.

death of her husband, Nawab Nazar Muhammad Khan, in 1819. This unorthodox arrangement seems to have been negotiated in response to factional fighting in the state at a time of political instability in central India, but it was confirmed when Qudsia proved herself to be an active and able administrator. Perhaps her best known project was a system of waterworks for the supply of clean drinking water to the people of Bhopal city, which, thanks to a perpetual endowment, continued to help fight waterborne diseases, like cholera, well into the twentieth century.[10] On the premature death of her own husband in 1844, Sikandar was able to call on this precedent to have herself named as regent for her infant daughter, Shah Jahan (1838-1901), subsequently using the opportunity, as Mrs Willoughby-Osborne's comment suggests, to demonstrate her own political and administrative acumen. Not only did she patronise religious and cultural activities, but she also reformed the revenue and judicial systems, military and police forces, transport, education and civil administration within Bhopal.[11]

[10] For discussion of Qudsia's administrative projects, see Sultan Jahan Begum of Bhopal, *Hayat-i-Qudsi: Life of the Nawab Gauhar Begum alias The Nawab Begum Qudsia of Bhopal*, tr. W.S. Davis (London: Kegan Paul, Trench, Trubner & Co Ltd. 1918), ch. 14.

[11] Her Highness the Nawab Shah Jahan of Bhopal, *The Taj-ul Ikbal Tarikh Bhopal; or, The History of Bhopal*, tr. H.C. Barstow (Calcutta: Thacker, Spink and Co., 1876), p. 58; Her Highness Nawab Sultan Jahan Begum of Bhopal, *An Account of My Life*, tr. C.H. Payne (London: John Murray, 1910), pp. 8-15.

Her prudence in the eyes of the British was confirmed by her actions during the large-scale military and civilian rebellion of 1857—referred to by Mrs Willoughby-Osborne, as in later colonial historiography, as the 'Sepoy War' or 'Indian Mutiny'. Though it was characterised by the British as a 'Muhammadan Conspiracy', there were several Muslim princes, including the Nizam of Hyderabad, who chose to remain uninvolved in this uprising on the basis that it was perceived by them to be led by their former Maratha enemies.[12] Sikandar also seems to have taken this line, suppressing the mutinous forces within Bhopal, offering refuge to British civilians in the region, and providing troops to aid the British cause outside of the state, despite her own mother and the Bhopal *'ulama* (religious scholars) encouraging her to rebel.[13] In the Queen's Proclamation of 1858, this loyalty on the part of the princes was richly rewarded with a guarantee that their treaties would be duly respected in future. Sikandar was also recognised individually, subsequently being granted the title of Nawab that enabled her to rule Bhopal in

[12] Sugata Bose and Ayesha Jalal, *Modern South Asia: History, Culture, Political Economy* (London: Routledge, 1998), p. 91.

[13] For a succinct account of 'the Mutiny' in Bhopal, see Shaharyar M. Khan, *The Begums of Bhopal: A Dynasty of Women Rulers in Raj India* (London: I.B. Tauris, 2000), pp. 97-102. Also useful is the introduction to K.D. Bhargava, *Descriptive List of Mutiny Papers in the National Archives of India, Bhopal* (New Delhi: National Archives of India, 1960).

her own right from 1860, as well as a nineteen-gun salute, the return of territory lost to a neighbouring prince and the Grand Cross of the Star of India.[14] Interestingly, this latter honour made her, at the time, the only female knight in the British Empire besides Queen Victoria, a position that underlines her unique status, as well as her close relationship with the British—a connection much vaunted by her successors.[15]

Sikandar has also been celebrated by her descendants on account of being the first Indian ruler, male or female, 'from the most powerful emperor down to the smallest chieftain,' to make the pilgrimage to Mecca.[16] At least part of their approbation seems to be due to the extremely perilous nature of this journey before the mid-twentieth century by which the prevalence of fatal illnesses, armed bandits, tribal wars, corrupt officials and transportation mishaps meant that many hajjis—including some of Sikandar's own party—simply did not return.[17] Even the greatest of the great Mughals, the emperor Akbar, had been discouraged from

[14] Sambhu Chandra Mukhopadhyaya, *The Career of an Indian Princess: The Late Begum Secunder of Bhopal, K.S.I.* (Calcutta: Anglo-Sanskrit Press, 1869), p. 10-11.

[15] Sultan Jahan, *Account*, 10. For this honour, Sikandar was also celebrated in the contemporary British press. See 'The Begum of Bhopal,' *Illustrated London News* (London), 16 May 1863.

[16] Khan, *Begums*, p. 108. See also Shah Jahan, *Taj-ul Ikbal*, p. 102; Sultan Jahan, *Account*, p. 17.

[17] For an account of the perils faced by hajj pilgrims in the late nineteenth century, see the appendix to *The Mecca Pilgrimage*

performing the hajj with his aunt, Gulbadan, and other female relatives in the 1570s on account of the length and danger of the journey.[18] That his womenfolk went anyway suggests that travel for the purpose of pilgrimage had long been an accepted pursuit for Indian women. Their numbers may, therefore, be presumed to make up a reasonable percentage of the five to seven thousand that, according to William R. Roff's estimates, departed on hajj from India each year in the mid-nineteenth century—numbers that were perhaps boosted in 1863 when Sikandar went with her party of nearly a thousand.[19] Of course, these figures are still a far cry from the two to two and a half million from around the world that go annually today, a change that may be attributed at least in part to improvements in transportation that were just beginning in Sikandar's

(London: Thos. Cook & Sons, 1893), pp. 13-19. It consists of an article originally written by a 'gentleman who has for several years been engaged in the Pilgrim trade as commander of a steamer' for *The Times of India*, 9 November 1885. Even in the 1920s when statistics first became available, death rates during hajj sometimes reached 13 per cent. Mary Byrne McDonnell, 'Patterns of Muslim Pilgrimage from Malaysia, 1885–1985' in Eickelman and Piscatori, *Muslim Travellers*, p. 114.

[18] Annette S. Beveridge, 'Introduction' to Gul-Badan Begam, *The History of Humâyûn (Humâyûn-nâmâ)*, third reprint (first published 1902) (Delhi: Low Price Publications, 1996), p. 69.

[19] Quoted in Michael N. Pearson, *Pilgrimage to Mecca: The Indian Experience 1500-1800* (Princeton: Markus Wiener Publishers, 1996), p. 54; Shah Jahan, *Taj-ul Ikbal*, p. 102.

time—the first railway line in India, for instance, had only been laid a decade before her departure.[20]

The numbers participating in the hajj in the nineteenth century also highlight that, whereas pilgrimage had taken on distinctly metaphorical connotations by this time in Europe, it remained among Muslims then, as now, a spiritual journey with a prescribed form: a scripted visit to the Ka'aba in Mecca undertaken at an assigned time in fulfilment of the requirements of the Islamic faith.[21] Of course, that is not to say that Muslims did not undertake other forms of pilgrimage as well. Indeed, it has been noted how visitations to shrines, a practice known as *ziyara*, retained their popularity in India in the modern period with the tombs of Sufi saints, like Shaikh Muinuddin Chishti at Ajmer, Shaikh Nizamuddin Auliya in Delhi and Baba Farid at Pakpattan in the Punjab, offering an important source of political and religious authority, despite opposition from religious reform movements with their emphasis on scripture.[22] Yet only hajj was obligatory, a point that reflects on issues of motivation, as well as perceptions

20 This argument has been made in the Malaysian context by McDonnell, 'Patterns', p. 114.

21 For an introduction to these rites and rituals, see Gustave E. Von Grunebaum, *Muhammadan Festivals* (New York: Henry Schuman, 1951), pp. 15-49.

22 See, for instance, Richard M. Eaton, 'The Political and Religious Authority of the Shrine of Bâbâ Farîd' in his *Essays on Islam and Indian History* (Delhi: Oxford University Press, 2000), pp. 203-24.

of 'centre' and 'periphery' within the Islamic world. Most Indian Muslims, as Michael Pearson has noted with regard to South Asian experience of hajj in the early modern period, went on pilgrimage accepting that Mecca was 'the source of correct Islamic doctrine and conduct', with the effect that most experienced an 'increase in orthodoxy' as a result of their journey, though some remained unchanged in their religious practice or, indeed, were inspired to 'greater tolerance'.[23] How this Muslim journey was written about in the colonial environment of British India will be explored in the following section.

Writing a Muslim Journey in a Colonial Environment

In her article on South Asian accounts of the hajj, Barbara Metcalf has charted the emergence of this genre from the eighteenth century, suggesting that it is very much a 'modern phenomenon'.[24] She makes this point on the basis that pre-modern South Asian Muslims were curiously silent about their experiences on hajj, even when they took the time to prepare their memoirs. The aforementioned Gulbadan, for instance, made no mention of her seven-year pilgrimage to the Hijaz in her narrative account of the reigns of her father, brother

[23] Pearson, *Pilgrimage*, ch. 3.

[24] Barbara D. Metcalf, 'The Pilgrimage Remembered: South Asian Accounts of the Hajj' in Eickelman and Piscatori, *Muslim Travellers*, p. 86.

and nephew, the Mughal emperors Babur, Humayun and Akbar, instead leaving it to court historians to record the most basic of itinerary.[25] The late Victorian translator of her work, Annette Beveridge, commented on this omission in her introduction to the English version with a sense of frustration clearly recognisable to any historian:

> How interesting it would have been if our princess had told us what it was in her heart that carried her through the laborious duties of piety she accomplished during her long stay in her holy land! She might have given us an essential principle by which to interpret the religious meaning which devout women attach to the rites commanded on the pilgrimage.[26]

Interestingly, this lack of introspection has been interpreted to be a feature of autobiographical writings in the medieval Islamic world more generally, despite a

[25] Abul Fazl, *Akbar-nama*, vol. III, tr. H. Beveridge (Calcutta: Asiatic Society, 1939), pp. 569-70.

[26] Beveridge, 'Introduction', p. 72-3. Gulbadan's omission may be contrasted with a highly emotive hajj account written in poetic form by a widow from Isfahan in the late seventeenth century. According to Kathryn Babayan, this 'singular female expression of sorrow' takes the form of a 'mystical journey toward God' that 'reveals how piety and life experiences kindled her desire to circumambulate the Ka'ba'. See '"In Spirit We Ate Each Other's Sorrow": Female Companionship in Seventeeth-Century Safavi Iran' in Kathryn Babayan and Afsaneh Najmabadi (eds.), *Islamicate Sexualities: Translations across Temporal Geographies of Desire* (Cambridge: Harvard University Press, forthcoming).

few exceptions.[27] From a Muslim perspective, the assumption seems to have been that, as hajj takes a prescribed form, there was little need to record what went on there beyond perhaps the receiving of visions or the advancement of Islamic knowledge.[28]

There is some debate among historians as to when the first hajj narrative was produced in the South Asian context. Metcalf follows the example of most Indian writers in attributing it to Maulana Rafiuddin Muradabadi, a disciple of the renowned hadith scholar and Delhi reformer, Shah Waliullah, who had gone on pilgrimage in 1787 and later wrote an account of it.[29] Challenging this perspective is Pearson who claims that another had appeared over a century earlier by the hand of a certain mullah called Safi bin Wali Qazvini.[30] Either way, what is clear is that there were very few accounts, whether in the form of published travelogues, journals or letters, before the publication of Sikandar's narrative in 1870. After that time, however, they began to

[27] Gustave E. Von Grunebaum, *Medieval Islam*, 2nd ed., (Chicago: University of Chicago Press, 1952), p. 275. For an exception, see Stephen F. Dale, *The Garden of the Eight Paradises: Bâbur and the Culture of Empire in Central Asia, Afghanistan and India (1483-1530)* (Leiden: Brill, 2004).

[28] Pearson, *Pilgrimage*, p. 17; Barbara D. Metcalf, 'What Happened in Mecca: Mumtaz Mufti's "Labbaik"' in Robert Folkenflik (ed.), *The Culture of Autobiography: Constructions of Self-Representation* (Stanford: Stanford University Press, 1993), p. 152.

[29] Metcalf, 'Pilgrimage Remembered', p. 86.

[30] Pearson, *Pilgrimage*, p. 16-7.

proliferate with 'several dozen' appearing between then and 1950 and 'ever more' after that, according to Metcalf's judgement.[31] What this suggests is that the impetus to write hajj accounts, like that to write novels, memoirs, biographies and other forms of modern literature, was closely related to the establishment of colonial rule in the Indian subcontinent, as well as the introduction of certain types of technology, most importantly the printing press. It has been noted already that Sikandar Begum had close connections with the British in India, and her familiarity with European ways is also evident from the text—a reference to some people in Jeddah riding donkeys astride, while others 'sit sideways as European ladies ride', providing just one example.[32] This text, then, provides further evidence of Metcalf's findings that it was those Muslims involved with colonialism who wrote pilgrim narratives on the basis that it was they who sought to contest and negotiate the 'multiple cultural values' with which they were familiar against the seemingly fixed 'cultural symbol' of the hajj.[33]

The influence of contact with Europeans on this process may also be seen in terms of the motivation to write. Sikandar Begum states explicitly on the first page of the first chapter of her narrative—the point having already been drawn out in the translator's preface—that

[31] Metcalf, 'Pilgrimage Remembered', p. 86.
[32] Sikandar, *Pilgrimage*, p. 36.
[33] Metcalf, 'What Happened in Mecca', p. 152.

she began the process of writing about her pilgrimage 'in compliance with a request'.[34] This request came, significantly, in written form even before she had departed in 1863, from Lady Durand and her husband, Colonel (later Major General Sir) H.M. Durand, formerly political agent in Bhopal, but, by then, foreign secretary of the Government of India.[35] Viewed within the context of the increasingly asymmetrical power relations of the 'subsidiary alliance' system, this seemingly informal appeal may almost be interpreted as an order. The appropriateness of this interpretation is supported in that the request involved Sikandar offering not only an account of what went on in Mecca, but also 'impressions of Arabia generally'.[36] The eliciting of this information could be understood to be an innocuous interest in foreign climes on the part of the Durands, but, equally so, it may have reflected a political motivation at a time when this region was viewed as a legitimate imperial aspiration, the British having already established a

[34] Willoughby-Osborne, 'Translator's Preface'.

[35] It may be surmised from a speech given by Major (later Colonel) G.B. Malleson at the Dalhousie Institute in 1865 that this written request came in the form of reply to an earlier letter from Sikandar. Apparently, she had written to Durand before departing on her journey in order to 'solicit forgiveness' for any offence that she may have caused him during his five or six years in Bhopal. Her intention was to leave on pilgrimage 'with as much purity as possible'. 'The Begum of Bhopal', *The Times* (London), 11 April 1865, p. 6.

[36] Sikandar, *Pilgrimage*, p. 2.

protectorate in southern Yemen in 1839.[37] At the same time, however, it should be noted that the way in which Sikandar abdicates responsibility for writing to the Durands evokes what Metcalf has called, a 'convention of passivity' within the long tradition of recording life stories and journeys within Islam. Just as a hajji must be 'called' to go on hajj, so must Sikandar portray herself as responding to someone else's invitation to write about it.[38] Thus, even while being inspired by the colonial milieu, her narrative retains an essentially Muslim characteristic.

The importance of the colonial context is also evident in that Sikandar's published work was very clearly directed at a British—or at least British in India—audience. The most obvious indication of this intended readership was that it was first published and then later republished in English by British publishers in London and Calcutta, but never appeared, as far as can be seen, in the original Urdu of the manuscript, although it was kept 'bound in quatro' by the royal family in Bhopal, at least until the late nineteenth century.[39] Later on in the

[37] For this background, see Ira Lapidus, *A History of Islamic Societies*, 2nd ed. (Cambridge: Cambridge University Press, 2002), p. 570.

[38] Metcalf, 'What Happened in Mecca', pp. 156-7.

[39] Shah Jahan, *Taj-ul Ikbal*, p. 102. Sikandar's later descendants make no mention of this original manuscript, nor has it been located through my own searching in either family collections in India or Pakistan or the National of Archives of India in Bhopal. These omissions suggests that it, like many other documents in Bhopal—notably, a diary written by the founder of the dynasty, Dost

twentieth century, this language of publication might have been interpreted as an attempt on the part of the author to reach across religious and national boundaries within South Asia to a subcontinental wide audience.[40] But in 1870, English was understood by too few Indians—not even Sikandar herself—to have fulfilled this purpose, despite having been famously adopted as the language of elite education, government and the higher courts by the utilitarian governor general, Lord William Bentinck, under the influence of his law minister, Thomas Babington Macaulay, in 1835.[41] To publish the narrative only in English implicitly placed Sikandar apart from other Muslims in South Asia, not least traditional Muslim elites, in favour of fulfilling what Eickelman and Piscatori have identified as 'the British image of the good and loyal Muslim'.[42]

As noted above, the English text also drew a number

Muhammad Khan (1672-1728)—may have been lost, perhaps during the tumult that accompanied Indian independence or on the death of the last ruling Nawab, Hamidullah Khan, in 1960. For a later reprint in English, see The Nawab Sikandar Begum of Bhopal, *A Pilgrimage to Mecca*, tr. Mrs Willoughby-Osborne (Calcutta: Thacker, Spink and Co., 1906).

[40] I have made this argument with reference to the memoirs of Sikandar's great great granddaughter, Princess Abida Sultaan of Bhopal, published in English in 2004. See my 'Introduction: A Princess Revealed' in Abida Sultaan, *Memoirs of a Rebel Princess* (Karachi: Oxford University Press, 2004), p. xvii.

[41] Literacy rates as a whole were only just over four per cent according to the census of 1881.

[42] Eickelman and Piscatori, *Muslim Travellers*, p. 6.

of parallels in describing what the ruling Begum observed in Arabia with European practices, thus making it intelligible to a British readership. Perhaps Sikandar was thinking of Lady Durand herself when she remarked that the Georgian wives of the Sherif of Mecca wear 'very small, fine handkerchiefs' on their heads such as 'English ladies carry in their hands'.[43] Conveniently, many of the references to money and costs were also converted from the currencies of Arabia into the more fathomable rupees and pounds.[44] One might also conclude on the basis of their nature and content that the book's two appendices were also intended for a British audience. The first is a 'sketch' of Bhopal history, perhaps adapted from an imperial gazetteer or summarised from one of the many books written by British officers on the 'native states' at this time, in which the exploits of the Sikandar and her predecessors were briefly recounted—with a strong emphasis on their relations with the British in India—for those unfamiliar with this 'loyal' state.[45] The second is a 'descriptive list of the holy places of Arabia' in which well over a hundred sites are detailed, some with

[43] Sikandar, *Pilgrimage*, p. 107.

[44] See, for instance, ibid., p. 36.

[45] Ibid., pp. 105-126. For comparison, see Major William Hough, *A Brief History of the Bhopal Principality in Central India* (Calcutta: The Baptist Mission Press, 1845); and Colonel G.B. Malleson, *An Historical Sketch of the Native States of India in Subsidiary Alliance with the British Government* (London: Longmans, Green and Co., 1875).

reference to Sikandar's experience of visiting them, though certainly not all. Translated from Urdu by the Chaplain of Sehore and dated according to the Muslim calendar, one may assume that it was drafted by a Muslim scholar well-versed in the religious practices and early Muslim history of the Hijaz—perhaps the ruling Begum's *diwan* (chief minister) and influential theologian, Maulvi Jamaluddin Khan. Yet, in its method of ordering and classifying the data, it could just as easily have been the work of an Enlightenment thinker, an observation that again highlights the process of negotiation involved in producing Muslim literature in a colonial context.

Yet another sign of the intended British audience were the illustrations, which included 'views' of Bhopal, as well as a photograph of the author herself (see frontispiece). This latter feature in particular is very rare in South Asian accounts of hajj, most likely on account of the common suspicion with which iconography tends to be viewed in Muslim cultures.[46] In this connection, it is also worth noting that in the photograph, Sikandar does not appear in *ihram*, the dress of the pilgrim, or even modestly veiled, as may befit a good Muslim woman. Instead, she is crowned, enthroned and flanked by bearers, proudly wearing on her chest what appears to be the medal bestowed upon her by the British government, complete with its portrait of the Queen-

[46] Metcalf, 'Pilgrimage Remembered', p. 100.

Empress.[47] Alongside it at the beginning of the publication is a dedication to Queen Victoria followed by a letter of thanks from Sikandar's daughter, Shah Jahan, who had succeeded her as Nawab Begum of Bhopal upon her death in 1868. Contained in its lines was effusive praise for the English monarch for having brought 'undisturbed tranquillity' to the 'Empire at large', as well as a hint of the practical considerations behind her stance: 'that my descendants may merit, as their ancestors did, the favour of the British Government'.[48] Sikandar's reputation for loyalty, as established during the 'Sepoy War', was thus on show to be admired by British readers—as, indeed, it often was in the contemporary British press.[49] As Sikandar herself noted towards the end of her narrative, however, the same reputation earned her very few favours and, more often, animosity from her fellow Muslims in the Arabian peninsula, notably the Sherif and Pasha of Mecca and the Pasha of Jeddah.[50]

47 Sikandar, *Pilgrimage*, frontispiece.

48 'Letter from H.H. Shah Jahan Begum, present Ruler of Bhopal, to Mrs Willoughby-Osborne, on hearing of Her Majesty's most gracious acceptance of the Dedication of the following Narrative' in Sikandar, *Pilgrimage*.

49 For just one example, see 'The Capital of India', *The Times* (London), 14 December 1868, p. 10. Unfortunately, no evidence has been found, either in the form of full reviews or passing comments in other sources, as to how the book was received by its intended British audience.

50 Sikandar, *Pilgrimage*, p. 127.

The matter of the dedication, not included until after Sikandar's death and apparently at the initiative of Mrs Willoughby-Osborne, raises the question of the latter's influence over the final form and content of the published work. The assumption may be that she had a fairly crucial role in determining the additional elements to be included, as well as the structure and even meaning of the text, especially if one considers that she is recognised on the title page as having 'edited', as well as translated, the work. The extent of her intervention also seems to be suggested by Shah Jahan's comment in her own history of Bhopal, that her mother's manuscript was just a diary kept during her travels until the wife of the political agent converted it into publishable form.[51] This judgement conflicts, however, with Sikandar's own assertion that the narrative was penned upon her return—in 1867, according to the translator's preface.[52] In this context, Mrs Willoughby-Osborne also records that the only 'license' that she allowed herself in translating the manuscript was the 'occasional transposition of a paragraph', deemed necessary on account of the 'wholly unstudied' nature of the draft, it having been 'compiled' from 'rough notes' made during the journey.[53] There is evidence of this type of intercession in the body of the

51 Shah Jahan, *Taj-ul Ikbal,* p. 102

52 Sikandar, *Pilgrimage*, p. 2; and Willoughby-Osborne, 'Translator's Preface'.

53 Willoughby-Osborne, 'Translator's Preface'.

work; for instance, in a footnote in the first chapter in which the translator comments that she has moved a paragraph on 'preparatory religious observances' for the hajj from the end of the Begum's manuscript to the beginning on the basis that this was a 'more appropriate position for it.'[54] This remarks points to the way in which she felt it necessary to enforce at least a rough chronology on Sikandar's narrative.

It seems fair to conjecture that Mrs Willoughby-Osborne was also responsible for the insertion of chapter breaks—though these are only numbered, not named—on the basis that some of them at least seem to interrupt what is otherwise a continuous narrative. Consider, for instance, the concluding line in chapter XIII in which Sikandar asserts that she would 'now proceed to describe' her visit to the Sherif of Mecca only for the chapter to end abruptly. The subsequent chapter then begins with the apparent sequitur: 'I went on foot to the Sherif's house...'[55] Beyond this, the translator's impact on the published narrative actually seems to have been fairly limited, even in terms of the meaning of the text. Indeed, she makes the point in her preface that she has 'endeavoured to adhere to the literal meaning of the Urdu as closely as possible'.[56] And, where there was confusion due to literary convention,

54 Sikandar, *Pilgrimage*, p. 2, fn.

55 Ibid., pp. 104-5.

56 Willoughby-Osborns, 'Translator's Preface'.

she tended to include literal translations in brackets. In a section on the climate in Mecca, for instance, she translated the Begum's words as 'the heat had been intense (lit. "it had rained fire").'[57] Elsewhere, she went so far as to include lines of transliterated Urdu text.[58] That is not to say, of course, that certain aspects of the original have not been lost through the rendering of this narrative into English. At the least, it denies us the opportunity to undertake the careful analysis of language in terms of vocabulary, grammar and tense that has proved so revealing of cultural personality, political identity and social attitudes in, for instance, Stephen Dale's thoughtful study of the autobiographical writings of the Mughal emperor Babur.[59]

In terms of style and structure, it seems that Mrs Willoughby-Osborne also did not make too many changes. Though the narrative is, on the whole, sequential in nature, it remains interspersed with thematic interludes that discuss specific problems faced and locations observed, with little regard for the constraints of chronology. The entire second chapter, for instance, is dedicated to the ruling Begum's wranglings with the customs authorities in Jeddah as they occurred both at the beginning and the end of her stay in Arabia. The author herself signals this shift in context by making reference to goods being sent from Mecca to Jeddah,

[57] Sikandar, *Pilgrimage*, p. 64.
[58] Ibid., p. 35.
[59] Dale, *Garden*.

rather than Bombay to Jeddah, only to have it reinforced by the translator in a footnote in which she explained that the Begum was referring to 'what happened at a subsequent date'.[60] One is reminded of scholarly observations in relation to the renowned travel account, or *Rihla*, of the fourteenth century Moroccan traveller, Ibn Battuta (d. 1368-9), in which it is argued that he also 'combined reminiscences' from visits on the journey out and back, thus 'sacrificing chronology to literary neatness'.[61]

In the portrayal of time itself, a parallel may also be drawn with earlier Muslim travel writers. In the early chapters, there are regular references to the dates on which activities occurred, carefully documented according to the Islamic and Christian calendars, as in the case of the arrival of Sikandar's party at Jeddah 'on the 13th of the month Sh'aban, in the year of the Hejra 1280, corresponding to the 23rd January, 1864 of Christ'.[62] In the middle sections in which the Begum describes her residency in Mecca, on the other hand, the sense of time often seems to disappear, with very few

60 Sikandar, *Pilgrimage*, p. 21.

61 Tim Mackintosh-Smith (ed.), *The Travels of Ibn Battutah* (London: Picador, 2003), p.304fn12. On this issue of chronology in Ibn Battuta's *Rihla*, also see Ivan Hrbek, 'The Chronology of Ibn Battuta's Travels', *Archiv Orientalni*, 30 (1962), pp. 409-86; and Ross E. Dunn, *The Adventures of Ibn Battuta: A Muslim Traveller of the 14th Century*, rev. ed. (Berkeley: University of California Press, 2005), p. xiv.

62 Sikandar, *Pilgrimage*, p. 5.

dates or hours being provided to give a suggestion of the length of time involved in an activity or the periods between episodes. Where it does reappear, it is only with reference to a Muslim fast or festival—'the sacred month of Ramzán' or 'the second day of the 'Id-ul-Fitar'—or the rhythms of the Muslim day—'after mid-day prayers'.[63] This method of depicting time, along with the mixed form of organisation suggests the intermediate status of this work, sometimes displaying the qualities of modern literature, but sometimes harking back to earlier Muslim models.

The second chapter, as quoted in the previous paragraphs, is also useful for illustrating the way in which the 'rough' and 'unstudied' character of the original account, as alluded to by Mrs Willoughby-Osborne in her preface, was retained in the published version—suggesting, in turn, that she did little to smooth it out. This assertion is made on the basis that it, like many other sections as the story progresses, reads more like a collection of official correspondence than a coherent narrative. Consider the following opening lines from a series of paragraphs in this chapter:

> 'I then wrote to Mahomed Baksh, Deputy Harbour of Jeddah, to tell him that…'
> 'A letter came in answer from Shams-ud-dín, Custom House Officer, saying:…'
> 'To this Páshá 'Izzat Ahmed replied:…'

[63] Ibid., pp. 96, 103, 117.

> 'After this I again wrote to the Custom House Officer, saying:...'
>
> 'To this Shams-ud-dín replied:...'[64]

This literary method gives it the appearance of including dialogue, as one would find in a novel, thus conveying an 'immediacy of experience' that is, according to Metcalf, a feature of the most recent accounts from South Asia.[65] In this case, however, it does not seem to be so much a sign of modernity, as an attempt on the part of the busy Nawab Begum to recreate her story with as little effort as possible. Her haphazard approach to this task is borne out by the fact that the narrative has no real introduction, beyond the brief assigning of motivation, or conclusion. Indeed, the final chapter is simply another set of letters intended to provide evidence of why she did not travel to Medina, as well as Mecca, the main reasons cited being the dangers posed by the Bedouins, the poor quality of the route and the expense involved.[66] There is no retrospective on the journey as a whole, nor even an account of her return to India or events upon her arrival in Bhopal, though she does take a few pages in the second last chapter to 'recapitulate' her 'impressions of Mecca and Jeddah', seemingly in direct response to Durand's request.[67]

64 Ibid., pp. 7-12.

65 Metcalf, 'Pilgrimage Remembered', p. 95.

66 Sikandar, *Pilgrimage*, ch. XIX.

67 Ibid., pp. 129-32.

Interestingly, Sikandar's account also fails to include any reference to the initial journey from Bhopal to Bombay, assumedly taken partially by road and partially by rail, the reason being that Bhopal was not connected to the national rail network until 1884; or to the sea journey from Bombay to Jeddah, beyond an assertion that the author completed the 'prescribed religious exercises' en route.[68] These omissions may be explained on the basis that she did not feel the need to describe what would have already been familiar to her and her specified audience of the Durands. But it also gives the sense that 'discovering India' as part of a nationalist project at this very moment, when the concept of Indian nationhood was being forged, was not central to the ruling Begum's agenda in the way that it was to those members of the Bengali *bhadralok* writing travel narratives in the same period.[69] This observation raises the question of what, then, was her agenda—or leitmotif,

[68] Ibid., p. 4. This part of Sikandar's journey may, however, be recreated at least in part from contemporary news reports. See, for instance, articles on her arrival, departure and activities in Bombay in 'The Bombay Mail' section of *The Times* (London), 25 January and 6 February 1864.

[69] Kumkum Chatterjee, 'Discovering India: Travel, History and Identity in Late Nineteenth- and Early Twentieth-century India' in Daud Ali (ed.), *Invoking the Past: The Uses of History in South Asia* (New Delhi: Oxford University Press, 1999), pp. 192-227. On the travels of the Bengali *bhadralok*, also see Simonti Sen, *Travels to Europe: Self and Other in Bengali Travel Narratives 1870-1910* (Hyderabad: Orient Longman, 2005).

in the language of autobiography—in writing: was it, as one may perhaps expect of a pilgrim narrative, to chart her spiritual development as she undertook this grand journey of faith? Or did it have more mundane concerns? Was it, for instance, related to those political matters that proved so important in her motivation to write? And how did Sikandar express these notions of self and identity, especially at this point in history when the category of 'Indian Muslim', not to mention 'India' itself, was only just being constructed? These queries, as they provide insight both into the character of this narrative and the historical moment in which it was written, will be addressed in the following section.

Defining the Self against a Muslim Other

In his article on 'religious change and the self', Francis Robinson charts how Muslims in South Asia experienced a shift in terms of their understanding of the self from the nineteenth century, closely linked to their contact with European ideas in a colonial context and the spread of communications technology, among other factors. This change led to a much greater focus on what he terms, 'self-instrumentality', 'self-affirmation' and 'self-conscious-ness' in a way that heralded the emergence of a modern Muslim identity.[70] Barbara Metcalf has

[70] Francis Robinson, 'Religious Change and the Self in Muslim South Asia' in his *Islam and Muslim History in South Asia* (New Delhi: Oxford University Press, 2000), pp. 105-21.

drawn out this theme with regard to hajj narratives in particular, arguing that, increasingly, this genre became about 'representation of a self' and 'constituting a persona': less about the hajj and more about the hajji. According to this interpretation, we may expect more emphasis in 'modern' accounts on 'individual experiences, perceptions, and feelings' from authors who 'present themselves not only as observers but as active participants in what they describe'.[71] An illustrative example developed by Metcalf is that of the renowned Pakistani novelist and intellectual, Mumtaz Mufti, who first published his hajj account in book form in 1975. From the title alone—*Labbaik*—one gets a sense of the intimacy and immediacy of the described experience in that it means, 'I am here': the Arabic call of the hajji as he enters Mecca.[72] The opening sections in which this 'nominal Muslim' recounts a series of fantastical happenings—best exemplified by his idolatrous vision of the smiling face of Allah upon entering the Ka'aba itself—offer further evidence of the personal journey undertaken by the author.[73]

Written over a century earlier, Sikandar's account contains almost no trace of this spiritual soul-searching—even in a less unorthodox fashion—as she relates her pilgrimage to Mecca. Indeed, she rarely writes about

[71] Metcalf, 'Pilgrimage Remembered', p. 87.
[72] Ibid., p. 95. Also see Metcalf, 'What Happened in Mecca'.
[73] Metcalf, 'What Happened in Mecca', pp. 149-51.

spiritual matters at all, beyond recording in a list-like fashion that she completed various religious rituals as required. Even upon arriving at Mecca, a point when many pilgrims express their wonder at seeing the Ka'aba for the first time, she merely states with archetypal precision and briefness what happened, not what she felt or experienced:

> The hour of my arrival at Mecca was the 'Ishá (first watch of the night), and the call to evening prayers was sounding from the different mosques. I entered within the holy precincts by the Báb-us-Salám (gate of peace), and, arriving at the house of Abraham, I stood and read the prescribed prayers. After that, I performed the ceremonies of the Toáf-ul-Kudúm, and of running at the Safá and Marwáh.[74]

It is only thanks to footnotes directing the reader to the appendix, assumedly inserted by the translator, that we get any sense of what these activities entailed. She then returns to her preferred subject of the difficulties that she had in negotiating with the Sherif of Mecca, in this case for the rental of a house. Elsewhere, she discusses in great detail the arrangements involved in travelling to Arafat, Muzdalifah and Mina, but never explains why she was going or her reaction to this often challenging portion of the pilgrimage. There is a whole paragraph on the arrangements that were made for

[74] Sikandar, *Pilgrimage*, p. 46.

procuring guards, but only one line in which she makes reference to religious matters: 'I then proceeded to 'Arfát, and having completed the whole of the prescribed duties of the pilgrimage, I returned to the exalted Mecca.'[75]

Another point when the modern reader may expect a sense of spiritual reflection is upon Sikandar's completion of the hajj, but this moment, too, passes without any reference to her thoughts or feelings. To be sure, it is only mentioned at all in a description of a piece of correspondence from the Sherif of Mecca in which he offered his congratulations on the occasion of 'Id and, as if as an afterthought, 'of my having accomplished the pilgrimage'.[76] Much more attention was directed to the arrangements involved in holding a feast for the Sherif and the Pasha in commemoration of this event. Only on one or two occasions does the reader get a more explicit sense of the emotional investment involved in going on hajj from Sikandar's point of view. One such occasion was when she expressed her concern at being unable to complete a particular section of the hajj on account of her party repeatedly getting mobbed by crowds attracted by her mother's reputation for generosity to the poor. As she writes, 'I felt perfectly helpless, and began to question the utility of having gone to Mecca for devotional

75 Ibid., p. 125.
76 Ibid., p. 122.

ends.'[77] On the whole, however, one cannot help thinking that Annette Beveridge, that disappointed Victorian translator of Gulbadan's memoirs, would have been equally dissatisfied in not finding 'what it was in her heart' when this later Muslim princess completed the pilgrimage.

Yet, even if there is little overt exploration of the spiritual self in this narrative written on the cusp of modernity, there was, as perhaps already suggested, an implicit set of concerns that shaped the account. The reader becomes aware, through the way the Nawab Begum presented herself and others, of whom she understood herself to be. And, as with many hajjis travelling from British India in the late nineteenth century, it was, as Metcalf has noted, 'imperial issues' that were 'close to the surface of their perceptions'. She provides the example of Mirza 'Irfan 'Ali Beg, a deputy collector in the Indian Civil Service, who published an account in 1895 in which he reflected on his expectations for good government as they would impact on the emerging political category of the 'Indian Muslim'—specifically the provision of 'order, protection, comfort, and cleanliness'—directing his words both at the British government in India (to the point that he had his Urdu account translated into English) and the Turks in the Hijaz.[78] In a very similar fashion, Sikandar portrayed herself as every bit the reforming princess—the

77 Ibid., p. 84.

78 Metcalf, 'Pilgrimage Remembered', pp. 89-90.

'improving landlord' modelled on the estate-holders of Britain—that the imperial overlord expected her to be. Her ongoing critique of Arabia's officials—depicted in this narrative as corrupt and decadent as any 'Oriental despot' of the British imagination—demonstrates the degree to which she had internalised these ideals and become active in their reproduction.

A useful illustration of this theme can be found in a reported conversation between Sikandar and the Pasha of Mecca in which she expressed her opinions on administrative matters in an entirely forthright manner. When the Pasha informed her that the present Sultan of Turkey had a 'great liking' for 'cannons, guns, ships and road-making', she responded by asking if he had 'any railways or telegraphs in his country'. Upon being told not, she proposed that, as the latter was the 'most important' of 'all public works', he ought to instal one between Mecca and Constantinople.[79] Further evidence can be found in a section towards the end of the narrative in which Sikandar reflected on why the Sherif and the Pasha were, as noted above, so antagonistic towards her. She suggested that it might have been because one of the Pasha's servants had been present when she had proclaimed to her own party that the administration of the Hijaz was so poor that *she* should take over! It is worth quoting this passage at length in order to get a clear sense of her self-perception as it

[79] Sikandar, *Pilgrimage*, p. 119.

was inextricably entwined with British standards of good government:

> The Sultan of Turkey gives thirty lakhs of rupees (£300,000) a-year for the expenses incurred in keeping up the holy places at Mecca and Medina. But there is neither cleanliness in the city, nor are there any good arrangements made within the precincts of the shrines. Now if the Sultan would give *me* those thirty lakhs, I would make arrangements for the Government of Bhopal to be carried on by my son-in-law and daughter, and you would see what a state of order and cleanliness *I* would keep the august cities in, and what arrangements *I* would make for the proper maintenance of the holy shrines; so that the Sultan would find out that dishonest people had been diverting his money from its legitimate uses, and had not kept a single thing in order; while I, in a few days, would effect a complete reformation!

The faith of this Indian Muslim princess in her own administrative abilities still reads as surprising over a hundred years on. Even in recounting the story, she expressed no sense of humility or remorse: 'If he had been a man of liberal views, he would have been rather pleased than otherwise, and have asked me to explain what arrangements I thought were required.'[80]

[80] Ibid., pp. 127-28.

Related to this concern was Sikandar's consistent portrayal of herself as a frugal—and, hence, prudent—ruler. On a number of occasions, she reported how she had underestimated the expenses involved with her pilgrimage, not, for instance, being willing to pay the exorbitant customs duties at Jeddah or give gifts of expected value to the Sherif of Mecca. Even her decision not to go to Medina was influenced by these pecuniary matters as the following quotation illustrates: 'The Bedouins demand Bukhsheesh at every step, and if they do not obtain money or food, frequently grossly insult, or even kill one. Where am I to find money to satisfy all their demands?'[81] That is not to say that she was not generous with her charitable donations, as would be expected of a Muslim pilgrim, but she denounced the 'indiscriminate' nature of her mother's liberality.[82] At the same time, her narrative made it clear that she saw the world through a hierarchical lens with herself placed towards the top of the ladder of rank and status. In a section on methods of transport in Jeddah, to take just one example, she noted that 'people of rank' rode a particular type of camel and, hence, one had been hired

[81] Ibid., p. 134. Interestingly, Sikandar's account of the threat posed by 'Bedouin highwaymen' was supported by the above-mentioned article in *The Times of India*. It reported that, if pilgrims did not book their camels to Mecca with the 'Safe Carrying Company'—said to have an arrangement with the Bedouin—their safety could not be guaranteed. *The Mecca Pilgrimage*, p. 17.

[82] Sikandar, *Pilgrimage*, p. 135.

for her as well—though only after the price had been carefully negotiated.[83]

In her eschewing of extravagance, one may see the ruling Begum's identification with the Muslim socio-religious reform movement traced in the Indian context to the Delhi theologian, Shah Waliullah (1703-1763). Her association with this school of thought is also suggested by her attempt, during her stay in Mecca, to have the Qur'an translated into Turkish—'in order that those Turks who were unable to understand it in the original, might be acquainted with it by this means'—just as Shah Waliullah had translated it into Persian and his son, Abdul Qadir, into Urdu. She did so at the suggestion of her first minister, Maulvi Jamaluddin, who himself had studied with the descendants of Shah Waliullah in Delhi. Interestingly, the Pasha of Mecca actually forbade her from going ahead with this project on the basis that 'a translation of the Korán itself was not allowed'; if 'the lower orders' wanted insight into the holy book, he advised her, they could consult a commentary in Turkish instead. Predictably, she ignored his advice because it seemed 'adverse to the weal of the common people' and ordered the translation to go ahead anyway.[84] In doing so, she anticipated what was to become a central tenet of the pro-gramme of Turkish nationalists, like

83 Ibid.

84 Ibid., p. 88. On Shah Waliullah, see J.M.S. Baljon, *Religion and Thought of Shah Wali Allah Dihlawi 1703-1762* (Leiden: Brill, 1986).

Ziya Gökalp (1875/6-1924), in the early twentieth century.[85]

What is clear, then, from this narrative is that the differences between the Begum of Bhopal and the Sherif of Mecca or Pasha of Jeddah, as she understood them, were not just a simple clash of personalities or even Qur'anic interpretations. It was against this Muslim 'other' that Sikandar formed a sense of what it meant to be an Indian Muslim. Over and over, she reported the grievous misunderstandings that arose between her and Arabian officials over matters of custom—from her 'disgraceful' cash gifts on arrival (*nazar*) to their disconcerting habit of visiting without warning—to the point that she actually made the suggestion that officers be appointed on both sides to ensure that 'proper etiquette' was observed.[86] Yet it was language more than other issues that acted as an impenetrable boundary between the Nawab Begum and the people of Arabia. Not only did she complain repeatedly about not being able to communicate except through a translator, but she also issued an order at one stage that the guards only let into her quarters 'ladies who spoke Hindustani'.[87] The matter also arose in explaining why she did not complete the journey to Medina: 'I know nothing of Arabic, or of

[85] Niyazi Berkes (tr. and ed.), *Turkish Nationalism and Western Civilization* (London: George Allen and Unwin, 1959), p. 301.

[86] Sikandar, *Pilgrimage*, p. 59.

[87] Ibid., p. 83.

the language and customs of the Bedouins, so cannot understand what they say, or what they do.'[88] This statement highlights how Sikandar Begum, like the case studies in Eickelman and Piscatori's collection, might have come to Mecca expecting to be enveloped by a sense of Muslim solidarity, but certainly did not leave with it. On the contrary, she reveals a heightened sense of identity with her fellow Indian Muslims whom she, like Mirza 'Irfan 'Ali Beg, identified as a persecuted group in Mecca.[89] In light of this experience, it seems appropriate to investigate what her impressions were, more generally, of this 'other'. How did this Indian Muslim princess construct 'the Orient'?

An Alternative Construction of 'the Orient'

Edward Said's groundbreaking 1978 work, *Orientalism*, drew attention to the way in which Europeans had appropriated 'the East', crafting a vision of 'the Orient' by which 'Orientals' themselves—whether Turkish, Arabian, Indian or otherwise—had little power or control over their own self-depiction.[90] This idea was subsequently developed with regard to travel literature by authors like Mary Louise Pratt, who interpreted this genre as a device by which the imperial centre could

[88] Ibid., pp. 133-34.
[89] Ibid., pp. 29, 74.
[90] Edward Said, *Orientalism: Western Concepts of the Orient* (New York: Pantheon, 1978).

'present and re-present its peripheries and its others continually to itself'.[91] Yet to argue for this single hegemonising discourse denies the agency of anyone outside of Europe in creating knowledge about themselves or others. In response, Antoinette Burton has highlighted the way in which travelogues, letters and newspaper articles written by colonial subjects abroad may be read as 'complex and critical ethnographies' of the places they visited, in which Orientalist assumptions may be upheld, negotiated or contested depending on the author and historical moment. One of the examples that she provides is Cornelia Sorabji, mentioned in the introduction, whom she identifies as not fitting easily with the dialectic of either 'complicity' or 'resistance' in her depictions of Victorian Oxford and London, in that she employed certain tropes—like that of 'the Indian woman'—selectively in her articles and letters home as part of an elaborate strategy to enable her to 'survive the pressures' of attending Somerville College. To approach travel writing in this way allows us to appreciate, as Burton notes, 'how agency is possible while recognizing at the same time the constraints imposed upon it by structural determinants'.[92]

Sikandar Begum's narrative also has the quality of travelogue as ethnography, perhaps especially so in that

[91] Mary Louise Pratt, *Imperial Eyes: Travel Writing and Transculturation* (New York: Routledge, 1992), pp. 1-11.
[92] Burton, *At the Heart of Empire*, pp. 3, 16-17.

she had, as noted in an earlier section, been asked to give her 'impressions of Arabia' by the Durands. Indeed, there are entire sections that would not seem out of place in the work of a social anthropologist. Consider, for instance, the lengthy passage in chapter XIV in which she describes her visit to the home of the Sherif of Mecca's seven wives. It provides a detailed record based on careful observation of the elaborate method of greeting (culminating with a touch of cheeks and a light kiss on the lips), the costumes worn (in particular, the satin dresses encrusted with jewels and the 'coquettish' headdresses of the Sherif's two Georgian wives) and the food served ('cups of coffee and pomegranate sherbet'), as well as the code of behaviour observed by the women, their servants and their visitors in relation to each other and the Sherif—how only those wives who had borne children were permitted to sit in the Sherif's presence, and the way in which servants kissed the chair of state, rather than the Sherif's hand or dress, as did visitors of greater or lesser importance.[93] Another representative section is one on slavery in which, over several pages, Sikandar explains how 'male and female slaves of all races' were bought and sold in the slave market in Mecca, as well as describing the duties completed and the treatment received.[94] The quality of her record is suggested in that the high-ranking colonial

[93] Sikandar, *Pilgrimage*, pp. 105-112.
[94] Ibid., pp. 77-9.

administrator and Arabist, Sir William Muir, subsequently used it as evidence of the continuation of domestic concubinage among Muslims in the second edition of his *Life of Mahomet*, published in 1877.[95] To be sure, her observations in these sections were, on the whole, recorded in an objective fashion that emphasised accuracy, seemingly in deference to a kind of scientific method, even as it revealed its debt to an Islamic literary mode of 'reportage'.[96]

There are also several chapters dedicated entirely to her 'impressions of Mecca and Jeddah' in which she comments on a wide range of subjects from confectionary and horses to weather, vegetables and windmills. In these sections, she casts her judgement more freely, giving valuable insight into her cultural reality. It becomes apparent immediately that there were certain features of Arabia that were to her liking: the horses were 'very handsome and well bred', the fruit 'better and sweeter' than that in India, the moonlight in Mecca 'magnificent' and the sweets of Jeddah 'well made'.[97] Other aspects elicited curiosity. The Arabian-style windmills, for instance, with their 'openings in the side', warranted a paragraph's description, as did the 'small pebbles of all

[95] See Avril A. Powell, 'Indian Muslim Modernists and the Issue of Slavery in Islam' in Indrani Chatterjee and Richard Eaton (eds), *Slavery and South Asian History* (Bloomington: Indiana University Press, 2006).

[96] On this, see Dale, *Garden.*

[97] Sikandar, *Pilgrimage*, pp. 32, 38, 130.

colours' on a hill outside Mecca.[98] Most aspects of Arabian culture, society and environment, however, elicits a harsh and critical reaction from the visiting Nawab Begum with the greatest invective saved for the Arab people. The majority of this group, she summarises, were, in terms of character, 'miserly, violent-tempered, hard-hearted, and covetous', not to mention 'awkward and stupid'.[99] She develops this critique throughout her narrative, providing ample examples of the bribes expected by officials, the cheating that went on between employers and employees, and the difficulties involved in 'buying and selling' when one could expect the tradesmen to 'spit in [your] face and insult [you]'.[100] There are even echoes of the European stereotype of 'lazy Arabs' in her proclamation that, in Mecca, 'it is no disgrace to any one to beg; high and low, young men and old, women, boys and girls of all grades, are more or less beggars… It seemed to me that begging was held to be as honourable as working'.[101]

The women of Arabia were, in particular, objects of her wrath; she found that they were 'noisy', 'large-made' and displayed 'greater muscular strength than the men'.[102] She also expresses disapproval of their habit of singing comic songs and dancing at weddings,

[98] Ibid., pp. 30-1, 74-5.
[99] Ibid., p. 132.
[100] Ibid., pp. 29-30, 71.
[101] Ibid., p. 71.
[102] Ibid., p. 131.

commenting that 'they do both so badly, that one had not the slightest pleasure in hearing or seeing them, but is rather disgusted than otherwise', following it up with the sardonic comment that amateur musicians of this kind in India 'practise it stealthily in their houses'.[103] These observations suggest that Arab women did not fulfil Sikandar's expectations of modesty and demureness from the 'weaker sex', as they were rooted in Indian patriarchal values and coloured by Victorian notions of domesticity—though one must remember that these criticisms were coming from a female ruler who had, in her younger days, taken part in a battle on horseback against her own husband! Reflecting this background, Sikandar's most vicious diatribe is directed against Meccan women's habit of contracting multiple marriages. Consider the scorn implicit in the following passage:

> Women frequently contract as many as ten marriages, and those who have only been married twice are few in number. If a woman sees her husband growing old, or if she happen[s] to admire any one else, she goes to the Shêríf, and after having settled the matter with him, she puts away her husband, and takes to herself another, who is perhaps young, good-looking, and rich. In this way a marriage seldom lasts more than a year or two.[104]

[103] Ibid., p. 70.
[104] Ibid., p. 72.

This description fed into Victorian ideals of companionate marriage, but it was also informed by the Bhopali ruling family's Afghan roots—reflected in the text in references to 'We, Afgháns…'—by which divorce and widow remarriage were not acceptable practices, regardless of what is said in the Qur'an.[105]

Another feature of Arabian society that garnered the especial attention of the ruling Begum were the sanitary arrangements. Upon arriving in Jeddah, for instance, the first observation that she makes is that, though it appeared 'from a distance' to have an 'imposing appearance', one was struck upon entering the city by the 'dirty aspect of the streets and their total want of drainage'—a point that she also makes repeatedly with regard to Mecca.[106] Elsewhere, she notes that Turks in particular are 'very dirty in their habits', both in terms of their 'very dirty' houses and 'untidy' dress.[107] Interestingly, she relates this lack of cleanliness to religious values in a section in which she records a conversation between herself and the Pasha of Mecca's son, Suliman Beg. Apparently, she had questioned him

[105] Ibid., p. 58. For comparison, see Sultan Jahan, *Account*, p. 103-4.
[106] Sikandar, *Pilgrimage*, pp. 27, 68. According to the above-mentioned article on hajj in *The Times of India*, this impression of Jeddah and Mecca was widespread among pilgrims. The author himself went so far as to proclaim that Jeddah was 'one of the most dirty and foul smelling places that I have ever met with during my 20 years travelling over this globe'. *The Mecca Pilgrimage*, p. 16.
[107] Sikandar, *Pilgrimage*, pp. 68-9.

as to why the people of Mecca wore 'very dirty clothes' when it was dictated by the Islamic faith that they should have 'clean clothes, a clean body, a clean spot to worship in [and] clean water for ablution'. Unsatisfied with his explanation that the Pasha could not afford to provide new clothes for all of the poor people that descended on Mecca, she advises that the problem could be more easily resolved if he simply employed more washermen and reduced the rate for laundry, as well as issuing a decree to his own servants and subjects that 'cleanliness is expected'. This statement reflects not only the Begum's projected image of herself as an admini-strative reformer as discussed in the previous section, but also the way in which her participation in a colonial discourse on sanitation was shaped by hygienic concepts central to indigenous systems of knowledge in the Muslim world.[108] In doing so, it was part of a proliferation of medical writings in India from the late nineteenth century that, as Guy Attewell has noted, blended Islamic principles relating to the functioning of the body with sanitation in its 'western medical connotations'.[109]

What also emerges from this quote is the way in which Sikandar's experience on hajj led her to reject Arabia—usually conceived, due to its proximity to the 'sacred space' of Mecca, as a place of 'greater sanctity

108 Ibid., p. 94.

109 Guy Attewell, 'Authority, Knowledge and Practice in Unani Tibb in India, c. 1890-1930' (Unpublished PhD Thesis, University of London, 2004), ch. 5.

and, thus, religious or political legitimacy', in the words of Eickelman and Piscatori[110]—as a centre of good Islamic practice. Not only did the people of this region disregard Islamic laws on cleanliness, but they also drank 'wine and other intoxicating liquors' strictly prohibited by the Prophet Muhammad, to her manifest surprise.[111] Disappointment was also expressed in relation to the quality of the Arabic spoken, the Begum noting that only a few expressed themselves in its 'pure' form, despite it being the language of conversation—though, in light of her professed ignorance of the language, it is not clear how she would have known. Regardless, her observations led her to conclude that, while urban dwellers knew 'something of religion', those who inhabited the mountainous regions were 'totally ignorant of it'.[112] Notions of 'centre' and 'periphery' within the Islamic world were, thus, reconfigured as a result of her hajj, with India no longer being relegated to *l'Islam périphérique*, to use the terminology of some French scholars.[113] One may fairly assume that Sikandar was not inspired to practise a more Arabian-style of Islam upon her return in the manner of those Mughal pilgrims discussed by Pearson. On the contrary, she constructed an image of 'the Orient' that reflected and contributed to a colonial discourse, but in terms that exhibited her

110 Eickelman and Piscatori, *Muslim Travellers*, p. 12.
111 Sikandar, *Pilgrimage*. p. 30.
112 Ibid., p. 73.
113 Eickelman and Piscatori, *Muslim Travellers*, p. 12.

composite identity as an Indian Muslim woman of Afghan descent who ruled, and wrote, within the constraints of the subsidiary alliance system.

'Viewing Things from an Oriental Point of View': Conclusions

It was noted in the opening section that one of the 'novel' aspects of Sikandar's hajj account as identified by its translator, Mrs Willoughby-Osborne, was that it offered a rare chance to 'view things from an Oriental point of view'. Analysing this narrative nearly a hundred and forty years on, the insightfulness of her words, particularly with regard to the study of travel and travel writing, are all the more evident. Here is a documentary record that provides unique insight into the factors that went into writing a Muslim journey in a colonial environment, the process by which notions of the self were redefined against a Muslim 'other', and the way in which Arabia was constructed by a colonial subject as part of a modernist discourse about 'the Orient'. It tells the story of an Indian Muslim princess as she underwent a journey 'at once inner and outer', to borrow the words of Barbara Metcalf,[114] redefining and reimagining her sense of self, home, away and other as she fulfilled an obligatory tenet of the Islamic faith. What emerges is a snapshot of a genuinely complex individual as she negotiated with the colonial power, her fellow Indians

[114] Metcalf, 'Pilgrimage Remembered', p. 85.

and her South and West Asian co-religionists to craft an image of herself as an effective administrator, a loyal subject and a good Muslim. In doing so, she produced an intermediary literary work that revealed its debt to a European presence in India—not least in the very act of writing this type of account—while preserving important features of the long tradition of recording journeys and life stories within Islam: passivity was retained, chronology was fluid, time was sacred and introspection was minimal. Even as it was inspired and influenced by the colonial milieu, so Sikandar's account of a pilgrimage to Mecca remained an essentially Muslim account of a quintessentially Muslim journey.

In drawing these conclusions, this case study seeks to highlight that there is much to be learnt from Indian Muslim women travellers in terms of the complex nature of cultural encounters within the context of world history. Not all had the same experiences; when Sikandar's own granddaughter, Nawab Sultan Jahan Begum of Bhopal (1858-1930; ruled 1901-1926), went on hajj in the first years of the twentieth century, she returned, in the words of a contemporary observer in her state, 'a much more ardent follower of the Prophet' and 'much more zealous in her own religion'.[115] Nevertheless, women and gender do need to be recognised, as Tony Ballantyne and Antoinette Burton have done very recently, for their 'constitutive role in

[115] Quoted in my 'Out of India', p. 268.

the shaping of global power and cross-cultural social organization', 'the politics of mobility and the mobility of politics', as they put it in a travel-related context.[116] These examples also provide further evidence of what Antoinette Burton has called elsewhere, 'colonial migrancy': the process by which people, goods and ideas 'criss-crossed' the globe in the colonial period, rather than being contained by the one-way flow between 'core' and 'periphery'—in this case, Britain and its colonies—implicit in the recurrent Victorian metaphor of the 'voyage out'.[117] Yet the historical experiences of non-European women travellers continue to be marginalised more often than not, just as they were in the otherwise fascinating exhibition at the National Portrait Gallery. Indeed, they find no place at all in *The Virago Book of Women Travellers*, nor Jane Robinson's charmingly-titled anthology of women's travel writing, *Unsuitable for Ladies*. In the introduction to the former, however, the editor does 'regret the absence of more multicultural voices' and express her hope that 'in the future these gender and racial gaps will be bridged'.[118] This book aims to take a step in that direction.

116 Ballantyne and Burton, *Bodies in Contact*, p. 7.

117 Burton, *At the Heart of Empire*, pp. 7, 10, 15.

118 Mary Morris with Larry O'Connor (eds.), *The Virago Book of Women Travellers* (London: Virago Press, 2004), pp. xxi-xxii; and Jane Robinson (ed.), *Unsuitable for Ladies: An Anthology of Women Travellers* (Oxford: Oxford Paperbacks, 2001).

A

PILGRIMAGE TO MECCA,

BY

THE NAWAB SIKANDAR

BEGUM OF BHOPAL, G.C.S.I.,

Translated from the Original Urdú, and edited by

MRS. WILLOUGHBY-OSBORNE.

FOLLOWED BY A

HISTORICAL SKETCH OF THE REIGNING FAMILY OF BHOPAL,

BY

LIEUT.-COL. WILLOUGHBY-OSBORNE, C.B.,

Political Agent in Bhopál.

And an Appendix

TRANSLATED BY

THE REV. WILLIAM WILKINSON,

Chaplain of Sebore.

LONDON:

WM. H. ALLEN & CO., 13, WATERLOO PLACE,

PALL MALL, S.W.

1870.

Dedicated by gracious permission to

HER MAJESTY QUEEN VICTORIA

PREFACES TO SIKANDAR BEGUM'S *A PILGRIMAGE TO MECCA*

Letter from H.H. Shah Jehán Begum, present Ruler of Bhopál, to Mrs. Willoughby-Osborne, on hearing of Her Majesty's most gracious acceptance of the Dedication of the Following Narrative.

After the usual compliments, "My dear Friend, I have, indeed, occasion to express my gratitude on hearing that Her Gracious Majesty has been pleased to accept the Dedication to herself of the book of travels in Arabia, written by the Nawáb Sikandar Begum, who is now in Paradise. The intelligence has given me, your friend, infinite pleasure, and had the late Nawáb Begum in her lifetime heard the good news, she would assuredly have testified her extreme gratification by declaring that she considered this honour one of the highest she had ever received.

The Great Creator of Heaven and Earth has called Her Majesty to be Empress of Hindustan, and for this act of His good providence I render to Him my heartfelt thanks. Under Her Majesty's equitable rule, crime has been repressed, more especially that of infanticide; the ruler, in common with her subjects, enjoys peace and comfort; and the Empire at large flourishes in undisturbed tranquility. My earnest prayer to Almighty God is that I may be enabled to show my unswerving loyalty to Her Majesty who is a great appreciator of merit, and the Fountain of Honour, and that my descendants may merit, as their ancestors did, the favour of the British govern-ment, and be considered the most faithful servants of the Crown.

"Your sincere Friend,

(Signed) "Shah Jehan,

"Begum."

TRANSLATOR'S PREFACE

"The following Narrative of Her Pilgrimage to Mecca, was written in 1867 by the Nawáb Sikandar Begum, of Bhopál, in compliance with a request from Lady Durand, whose husband, Sir H.M. Durand, K.C.S.I., had formerly been Political Agent at the Begum's Court. Only two copies were made: one for Lieut.-Col. Willoughby-Osborne, the present Political Agent in Bhopál. On perusing the narrative, it occurred to me that the story of a Pilgrimage written by a Mahomedan Princess, would not be without interest for the general reader, for the following reasons:

1stly. Because no work written by an Eastern lady has, that I am aware of, ever been published.

2ndly. Because only one of two European travellers have visited Mecca.

3rdly. Because the opportunity of viewing things from an Oriental point of view is a novel one. and

4thly. Because the Begum of Bhopál has earned for herself in India no inconsiderable reputation of sagacity, shrewdness, and enlightenment, and in England for her loyal attachment to the British Government during the troublous times of the Sepoy War.

I therefore solicited the Begum's permission to present her notes to the public in an English form.

The permission was readily granted, and in availing myself of it, I endeavoured to adhere to the literal meaning of the Urdú as closely as possible. The only license I have allowed myself has been the occasional transposition of a paragraph, for the narrative being compiled from rough notes made during the Begum's journey, was wholly unstudied.

The Begum died in November, 1868, while I was completing the last page of my translation; and as I was prevented by severe illness from translating the Appendix, I handed over this interesting portion of the work to the Rev. Wm. Wilkinson, Chaplain of Sehore, whose kind and cordial assistance I desire gratefully to record.

I am indebted to F. Fitzjames, Esq., Executive Engineer of Hoshungabad, for the greater number of the Photographs from which the illustrations are taken, and for the remainder to Captain Waterhouse, R.A.

In the translation of proper names, &c from the original, I have followed Sir Wm. Jones' system, except in the case of well-known words—such as "Mecca," "Begum," &c., &c.

E.L. Willoughby-Osborne

Bhopál Political Agency, Sehore,
January, 1869.

NARRATIVE

OF A

PILGRIMAGE TO MECCA.

In the Name of God, the Merciful and Compassionate!

CHAPTER I.

In the year of the Hejra, 1284, on the first day of Moharram,[1] corresponding to the 6th of May, 1864 of Christ, I received a letter from the wife of Colonel Durand,[2] foreign Secretary, from Simla, dated the 5th of the month of June, in the year of Christ 1863, in which she said: "If ever your Highness writes a description of your pilgrimage,

[1] Name of the first Mahomedan month, held sacred on account of the death of Husain, son of 'Alí, who was killed A.H. 61.

[2] Now Major-General Sir H.M. Durand, C.B., K.C.S.I. He was formerly Political Agent in Bhopál.

I shall be delighted to see it." And Colonel Durand also wrote, that "he was anxious to hear what my impressions of Arabia generally, and of Mecca in particular, might be." I replied that when I returned to Bhopál from the pilgrimage, I would comply with their request, and the present narrative is the result of that promise.

[1] Before leaving Bhopál for the pilgrimage, I performed the following religious exercises under the direction of Molvi[2] Abdúl Kaiúm. On the day appointed for me to leave my palace (the "Motí Mahal"), and the start on the pilgrimage, I first of all went through the prescribed ablutions (Wazú);[3] then I said two prayers (called Nafal, which are not enjoined but voluntary), and read some verses and

[1] This account of the preparatory religious observances on commencing the pilgrimage forms the *concluding* paragraph in the Begum's MS., but I have placed it here as a more appropriate position for it.

[2] Molvi—A learned man. In this case the Begum's religious instructor.

[3] Wazú—Ablution performed before prayer, consisting of cleaning the teeth, washing, first the hands, then the mouth inside, then throwing water on the forehead, washing the whole face, the arms, and lastly the feet.

invocations appropriate to the occasion, from the venerable Korán. I then left the house, and proceeded to the mosque of Mamola Sahibeh, which is near the palace, and went through the same ceremonies of ablutions, praying and reading. I then went to the Garden of Fazhat Afzá,[1] and remained there two days, receiving farewell visits, and transacting such state business as was pressing, and making final arrangements for my journey. After that, the day having arrived for me to leave that place, I went at the hour of evening prayer into the mosque in the Garden of Fazhat Afzá, and performed the same ablutions and religious exercises. From the mosque I proceeded to the hill of Futtehgarh,[2] and remained there the night, after having received more farewell visits. Next day, after ablutions, I drove to the tomb of the late Nawáb Nazír-ud-Daulah Nazar Mahomed Khán (the Begum's father), and offered a prayer for the repose of his spirit. After this I went to the tomb of my paternal grandfather, Nawáb

[1] The Begum's own garden.

[2] The fort at Bhopál, built by Dost Mahomed, founder of the Bhopal family, about A.D. 1721.

Wazír Mahomed Khán, and then to that of Nawáb Ghos Mahomed Khán, my maternal grandfather, and invoked a blessing on their departed spirits.

I then prayed for my own relations, and for all professing the Musalmán Faith, and I asked that a blessing might rest upon them from my act, that their absolution and mine might be secured, and that I might be permitted to return to Bhopál from the pilgrimage.

I now finally started on my journey to the exalted Mecca, and arriving at Bombay I embarked for Jeddah. At the time of the ship weighing anchor I read the prayers enjoined by Molvi Abdúl Kaiúm, and continued the prescribed religious exercises until the day of my arrival at Jeddah.

CHAPTER II.

On the 13th of the month Sh'abán, in the year of the Hejra 1280, corresponding to the 23rd January, 1864 of Christ, having made in company with my fellow pilgrims a prosperous voyage from Bombay, I arrived at Jeddah. Immediately after my arrival the Port Admiral of the Sultan of Turkey came on board, and said: "You cannot land to-day. After your arrival has been reported to the Shêríf and the Páshá of Mecca, you may be able to disembark to-morrow at about eight or nine o'clock and enter the city."

Accordingly, on the 24th January, at nine o'clock in the morning, the unlading of my luggage commenced; and accompanied by the Nawáb Kudsíah Begum,[1] Nawáb Mían Faujdár Mahomed

[1] Dowager Begum, mother of the Sikandar Begum.

Khán,[1] and Dr. Thomson,[2] I proceeded to the house of Ahmed 'Arab, where the caravan of pilgrims was staying. Here Dr. Thomson left me, and went to call on the Consul of Jeddah. Ahmed 'Arab received me very hospitably, giving a dinner in my honour, at which all the ladies of his family were present. We remained there, however, only until six o'clock in the evening, Ahmed 'Arab having informed me that a princess had arrived from Egypt, and would lodge at his house, and that therefore I must vacate it for her. I had no alternative but to do this; and I was consequently obliged to seek an asylum elsewhere; this I found at a house called Khúsh Shámiyán (Happy Dwelling).

Abdúl Rahím, the head of the caravan, went and asked Ahmed 'Arab to tell him what the charge would be for the three or four hours we had spent in his house; and the latter replied, that "As we had done him the honour to remain but a short time, he

[1] Uncle of the Sikandar Begum.

[2] Charles Thomson, Esq., M.D., Surgeon to the Bhopál Political Agency, who had been deputed by H.M.'s Indian Government to escort the Begum as far as Jeddah.

would receive no payment." Whereupon I made him a present of some bales of cloth, some coins, &c.

After all, the Egyptian princess never came, having found quarters elsewhere; and not only had we been put to much inconvenience, but Ahmed 'Arab was in no way benefited.

While the goods were being taken out of the ship, Nawáb Faujdár Mahomed Khán, who was present with the Kudsíah Begum, told her that her money chest had the cover broken, and that the rupees were scattered about. "Those Bedouin thieves," he added, "are scrambling for them."

The Kudsíah Begum replied, "If the box is broken the rupees are probably stolen. What is the use of your troubling yourself?"

On hearing this I became anxious about my luggage, and asked the people, "Why they were opening the boxes?" They replied, "that the custom dues might be paid."

I then wrote to Mahomed Baksh, Deputy Harbour Master of Jeddah, to tell him that "I had received a letter from the Governor of Bombay (Sir Bartle Frere, G.C.B.), informing me that 'the same dues which were exacted from British subjects would be demanded from me;' but that this letter was in Dr. Thomson's possession, and he would make it over to the Consul. Meantime I must inform him that the goods I had brought from Bhopál were not articles of commerce, but merely a year's supply of grain and clothes, also cooking vessels, and bales of cloth for the poor at the shrines of the exalted city of Mecca and august Medina; and that the jewellery consisted of offerings brought to bestow in charity. Therefore, having made an inventory of my unopened boxes, he should let me have them, and I would give him a list of what they contained. On my arrival at Mecca, the Shêríf of that place would compare the contents with the list I had given, and should there be any discrepancy the responsibility would rest with me. If the Shêríf would give me a statement of the dues, I would pay them, and if he would receive the money I should give it to him; or whatever the custom might be for British subjects, on being informed, I would act accordingly."

I also wrote to the same effect to Páshá 'Izzat Ahmed of Jeddah, and Shêríf Abdúlla of Mecca, adding: "That I wished to be informed of the arrangements they would make for the dues to be levied on my baggage."

A letter came in answer from Shams-ud-dín, Custom House Officer, saying: "Inasmuch as I am a servant of the Turkish Government and there are fixed custom dues for this port, I have no power to take less than the prescribed rates; but in consideration of your Highness having honoured this empire with a visit, and of the letter you refer to from the Governor of Bombay, and of his friendship towards you, also out of regard for our common faith, I will only examine one of your ten cases; be pleased, however, to send a list of the whole of your Highness' goods, that I may certify to its correctness, and receive the customs according to the above-mentioned regulations. And further, inform me of the name of your agent here."

Upon receipt of this I ordered Abdúl Karím "to make out copies of the lists I had given him, and hand them over to Háji Húsen, agent to Háji Ismáel-Bín-Habíb (of Bombay), in order that he might furnish copies to Mahomed Shams-ud-dín Effendí

(Custom House Officer), and to Dr. Thomson; but should the latter have sailed, his copy could be given to the Consul of Jeddah."

Abdúllah, Shêríf of Mecca, replied as follows: "The Custom House Officer is the person appointed by the Sultan of Turkey to attend to these matters. You must therefore ascertain from him the regulations that are laid down."

But wishing to take further advice from that high dignitary the Páshá of Jeddah, I caused a letter to be written to him on this wise:—"Your Excellency, whose disposition is full of kindness, only wishes to act justly, and I am persuaded, therefore, that you will spare me any unnecessary trouble, and devise the easiest plan of passing my goods."

To this Páshá 'Izzat Ahmed replied: "Although it is really the duty of the Custom House Officer to attend to these matters, and although on your arrival he sent you a letter stating the regulations laid down by this Government, yet with the view of explaining the purport of his letter more fully to your Highness, I send to-day my son, Núrehasham-Súlímán-Ásaf-Beg, with this reply; and I feel confident that, from the clearness of his explanation, your Highness will acquiesce in what has been already written, and that any cause of annoyance will be removed."

After this I again wrote to the Custom House Officer, saying: "With regard to what you state of your Government regulations, viz., 'That all the luggage must be examined, but that out of consideration of your friendship and regard for me, only one box out of the ten should be opened,' the fact of the matter is this—that they have taken away the list of all my goods which were on board the steamship 'Indore', after leaving everything in confusion. How, then, can I send the list to you? Of the remaining baggage which is coming on board the sailing vessel 'Abúshír Márjan', my agent, Hájí Húsen, will send you an inventory. Whatever dutiable things there may be, send me an account, and I will pay accordingly. As to opening the boxes, beyond creating confusion, I do not see what object is to be gained. In accordance with your letter I have appointed Hájí Húsen, agent of Seth Ismáel-Bin-Habib, to settle the payment of dues; but should he have left Jeddah, I can appoint another person."

To this Shams-ud-dín replied: "Send me the list of your goods (that are coming by the sailing vessel 'Abúshír Márjan,') in order that when the ship arrives I may take the packages out and compare them accordingly, thereby preventing injury to any of your Highness' property, which otherwise I should not be able to distinguish from that of others. The reason I wish for the list is that I may identify each package separately on landing; and I solemnly declare that I will carry out my promise, and beyond your personal property levy dues only on such things as may be liable to duty. As soon as your Highness arrived in the harbour of Jeddah, the goods (you had with you) were liable to duty, and you paid it voluntarily. I did not exact it unjustly. I told you then that at the unlading of the cargo I would only examine one box of the ten. I shall be much obliged, therefore, if you will furnish me with the list, and by the favour of Almighty God I will take every care, and place a guard over the luggage when it is landed. The prescribed dues will be exacted, and you need not trouble yourself further in the matter."

I had caused a similar letter to that sent to

the Custom House Officer to be written to Dr. Thomson, but as he took his departure very hurriedly, he did not return any answer, and simply made over the case to the Consul of Jeddah.[1]

Háji Abdúl Karím wrote to tell me that "he had given copies of the inventories to Dr. Thomson, and that he, in consequence of the absence of the English Consul at Jeddah, had taken them to the French Consul; and that after some preliminary conversation, they had entered into the following arrangement on my behalf: 'my luggage was not to be examined in the Custom House, but only the list was to be looked at; if there should be any doubt about the contents of the boxes, they were to be searched at the house I should be in. The French Consul agreed to make arrangements for me, and Dr. Thomson introduced to him Háji Húsen and Háji Ibráhím (Agents of the banker, Ismáel Bin Habíb), and said

[1] This hurried departure was unavoidable on Dr. Thomson's part. As the ship "Indore", which had been chartered by the Begum for the voyage to Jeddah, only remained there two days, and he had to return to Bombay in it.

that in his opinion it would be best for these two Hájís to transact all my business in Jeddah.' "

I ordered a letter to be written to Hájí Húsen, telling him that, "with regard to declaring the value of the goods as advised by Dr. Thomson, the fact of the matter was this—that of the things I was taking to the holy cities, there were no new ones; that my clothes had been in my possession ten or twelve years (how then could I declare their value?) that my jewels and plate might be forty or fifty years old, and their price was recorded in the Treasury at Bhopál. If I had the inventory with me, I would declare their value—that as I had not brought them as articles of merchandise, I could only say of what description they were."

I heard afterwards that it was the custom in this part of the world to make some sort of present to the Custom House people, if one wanted one's goods passed quickly. I therefore gave a shawl to Shams-ud-dín, but notwithstanding this, he and his subordinates did not act up to their engagements; for before communicating with me in the first instance, they had on the arrival of the "Indore", proceeded with the unlading of my boxes, and had exacted the dues. And besides this, they had completely upset and spoiled the luggage of the Kudsíah Begum and of the Nawáb Faujdár Mahomed Khán; in short, I concluded that my letter had arrived too late, but that on the arrival of the sailing ship "Abúshír Márjan," they would do as they had promised by letter.

But being anxious in the matter, I caused a letter to be written to Mr. Antonio de Silva (of Bombay), in which I complained: "That the Custom House people had not attended to the directions contained in the letter of the Governor of Bombay, and in fact would not listen to reason; for as soon as the goods reached the shore, they were tossed about in all directions, and nothing would satisfy these people but opening the boxes, searching, and exacting the dues." I added: "I write to you for this reason: that you may make arrangements, so that as soon as the ship 'Abúshír Márjan' casts anchor in the Harbour of Jeddah, the box containing the jewels brought for charitable purposes (i.e., for distribution among the poor at the holy cities of Mecca and Medina), may be opened, and the contents be distributed among the ladies of my suite; they will put them into their pándáns,[1] and the empty box, which is in the shape of a writing-case, can be passed as such, and as soon as the ladies reach the house, the jewels can be collected again and put into the box. The details of the matter will be explained to you verbally by Háji Abdúl Karím, the third agent. I have left him at Jeddah, and have not brought him on in my suite. He is well acquainted with the manners and customs of Arabia, and, whatever circumstances may arise, continue to act in concert with him. With respect to the boxes of clothes—in the first instance refuse to show them, but if they will not listen to this, then let the boxes be opened and shown. First, having conveyed the ladies to land in boats, accompany them to the house which I have engaged for them, and remain there. I have heard that it is not customary in Arabia to levy tolls on what ladies carry

[1] "Pándáns" are small bags carried by the natives of India, containing the spices and betel nut which they are in the habit of constantly eating.

on their persons. Mittú Khán (Senior Officer of Cavalry), and Hájí Abdúl Karím will attend to the unlading of the goods."

At last the ship arrived, and Abdúl Karím and Mr. Antonio de Silva carried out my instructions regarding the box of jewels, so *that* box escaped the dues. But as to the bales of cloth, and the provisions, I received the following account from Mittú Khán and Abdúl Karím: "To-day, being the 8th February, 1864, we disembarked the whole of your Highness' property with every care, under the direction of a person named Antonio de Silva. But the Custom House Officer would not hear anything that was said, and insisted upon opening all the bales and arbitrarily exacting the dues upon every article. The amount of trouble and annoyance we experienced is beyond description. He scattered all the things about; if a box chanced to be unlocked, well and good, if not he broke it open. In short, he spoilt all the cases and their contents. As yet we have been unable to discover what the particular tax levied upon each article may have been; apparently not a single thing has been exempted from dues. When we are informed on the subject we shall communicate with your Highness."

On hearing this I passed an order directing a copy of this letter to be sent through Háfiz Mahomed Khán to the Shêríf and Páshá.

Hájí Abdul Karím informed me, that "he had heard the duty on my bales of cloth and wearing apparel would amount to 150 or 200 Riáls (between £35 and £45), and that when he knew the particulars he would report accordingly."

The Páshá and Shêríf wrote that they were aware of Captain Mittú Khán being appointed to the charge of my property, and that any representation made by him to them, they would willingly attend to. They expressed regret at the conduct of the Custom House Officer, and said they had written to him on the subject, and that his reply should be forwarded to me.

Shams-ud-dín Effendi's letter to the Páshá was as follows: "I was ordered by you to show every respect and courtesy, consistent with Imperial regulations, to her Highness the Sikandar Begum in the examination of her property, and I am much astonished at hearing the complaint of her Highness' Agent, which was forwarded to me with your orders of the 7th Ramzán. I beg to state, with reference to these complaints, that I have already reported the course I adopted to insure her Highness receiving all due honour and respect. With the knowledge and concurrence of the Consul at Jeddah, and in the presence of the Begum's agent, I caused her Highness' property to be removed to a place of safety before examining it; out of eight boxes I only opened one, the remaining seven containing similar goods. The fact of the matter with regard to the box of shawls was this: I valued a box of shawls worth 5000 kurush (£45) at one-third of that sum, some of the shawls having been eaten in places by insects. I only opened one of the many boxes, said by the Begum's servants to contain jewelled trappings of her Highness' private horses; I did this to prevent the articles being thrown into confusion. I charged about 3000 kurush on certain things of value not required for daily use, and then permitted her Highness' servants, with all due courtesy, to remove the property; and no one seemed in the least annoyed. I now learn with great astonishment from Abdúl Karím that the Begum was much displeased. Why, I cannot conceive. I feel certain, if you will enquire of the Consul and of her Highness' Agent (who was present at the examination), that you will be satisfied of the truth of what I have written."

This is the account of what befell my own private property; I will now relate what happened in the case of that belonging to some of my suite. My personal servant, the mother of Adil Khán, wrote to inform me, that when her luggage was landed from the ship at Jeddah, the Custom House Officers seized a pair of bracelets she wore on her arms, and demanded a duty of seventy kurush (i.e., seven rupees) on them. The bracelets were made of silver gilt, and had only cost seven rupees. The Custom House Officials kept the bracelets for some time in their possession, and Adil Khán's mother consequently (on recovering the trinkets) sent them to me, requesting me to forward them to the Páshá, that he might see them and show them to some goldsmith; if they should prove to be of silver, the duty on silver should be exacted, but if of gold, the bracelets might be kept in lieu of duty.

On receiving this letter, I ordered a copy of the petition to be sent through Mahomed Husen, the Interpreter, and Captain Mittú Khán, to the Páshá, requesting him kindly to settle the case and to inform me of his decision.

After that I heard from Adil Khán's mother that the bracelets had been returned to her, through my prime minister, and that the duty had been refunded.

Regarding some boxes I sent from Mecca to Jeddah,[1] Hají Abdúl Kárím wrote as follows:—"Sheikh Mahomed, Agent of the Turkish steamer, and Abdúl Rahimán, Agent of Ibrahim Abdú Satar, will not take the box of State papers which is to be sent to Rajah Kishên Rám, the second Minister at Bhopál; they say it is too heavy, and that according to the tariff, they require on every 'díram' of paper, the sum of two kurush. At this rate, the box will cost fifty or sixty Riáls. I went myself to Sheikh

[1] The Begum is here referring to what happened at a subsequent date.

Mahomed, and said to him:—'These are merely papers and records to be sent to the State Paper Office at Bhopál. They are neither letters nor newspapers subject to the tariff you wish to enforce, contrary to Imperial regulations.' He replied—'If what you say be true, open the box; for unless I see the papers, I will not believe you.' Being helpless, I opened the box and showed them to him, and when he found I had spoken the truth he was ashamed of his conduct, and levied the proper duty of one Riál. To-day I put the box on board the steamer, after having carefully packed it and covered it with tarpaulin. Some boxes which arrived in charge of Mahomed (a head servant) to-day, were ordered by the Custom House Officer to be put near the door, awaiting examination. The Sepoy in charge of the property reported this to me, and I went myself and enquired the reason of this unnecessary trouble in the examination of the property. I said—'The boxes contain clothes and several jars of water from the well of Zamzam[1] at Mecca; but examine them.' He

[1] Hagar's well at Mecca.

then began to abuse me, and said—'You sent a false report to Her Highness of what happened when the boxes were landed from the Abúshir Márjan, and said I had broken the locks and spoiled the things in opening them. What did I spoil? I examined everything with the greatest care.' I replied—'I am no fool; as you treat Her Highness' property, so I will report of you.' He laughed and took my hand, saying,—'I am not in the least annoyed—I merely said you told a lie, as a sort of brotherly joke. The Páshá wrote and asked me why I had behaved so improperly when examining the Begum's property, and why I had not observed all due care and respect in the search? Now, what violence or want of courtesy did I show?' I replied—'Let bygones be bygones. Do what you consider necessary in the case of the goods now before you.' Upon this he seemed pleased, and told me to take away the boxes to my own house, for he did not want to examine them. I consequently took them away, and made them over to Mr. Antonio."

On receiving this letter, I caused one to be written to the Custom House Officer, telling him with my "salám," that fifteen days before I went on board, I would show him the boxes one by one previous to their being shipped. That I had merely come on a pilgrimage and not for trade, but that I should buy things to take away with me. That the boxes I might send from Mecca to Jeddah to the care of Mr. Antonio de Silva, the Custom House officials would be pleased not to open, and that they would abstain from giving my servants trouble—moreover that by constantly opening and closing the boxes the contents would be damaged.

Shams-ud-dín replied,—"I have received your Highness' letter, and according to your wishes, the things you are sending from Mecca to Jeddah shall be made over to your agent without any examination, because you are a guest of the Páshá. It is right, therefore, that I should comply with your wishes. When your Highness leaves Mecca for Jeddah, I shall be delighted to obey any orders you may send to me."

Mr. Antonio de Silva also wrote to inform me, that he, accompanied by Háfiz Mahomed Kárím, had paid a visit to the Custom House Officer, and had spoken about my property being examined, and that the latter had promised, whenever he was sent for, to go to him and examine my boxes.

I ordered that before the Custom House Officer examined the luggage, notice should be sent to the Consul at Jeddah, but that if no examination were required, the Consul should not be troubled.

To the Consul himself I wrote,—"I have sent my property on various occasions, by camels, from Mecca to Jeddah; and the Custom House Officer has declared that he must examine the boxes. I wrote and informed him that when I arrived at Jeddah I would allow him to see them before they were put on board. At that time I had engaged no ship, but now, thanks be to God! a vessel has arrived. I have therefore written to the Custom House Officer, and requested him to go to Mr. Antonio de Silva's and inspect my property beforehand. But I can get no definite answer from him. I send, therefore, his letter herewith for your perusal, and I shall feel excessively obliged by your kindly sending one of your subordinates with the Custom House Officer to Mr. de Silva's, and by your ordering him to examine such boxes as he may wish to see, before my arrival; also by your kindly ordering all my boxes, and the grain, &c., now lying at Jeddah, to be put on board at once, so that there may be no delay on my arrival. If the Custom House Officer does not wish to examine the things, make him distinctly say so. I bought nothing of value at Mecca, except some relics, &c. I hope you will do as I request, and send me a reply."

It appears that Shams-ud-dín, the Custom House Officer, did open my boxes, but finding in them only Zamzam water, antimony for the eyes, and relics, he allowed them to pass free of duty.

This is the account of all that happened in the matter of Custom dues, and of what befell the things I took in the steamer "Indore," and the ship "Abúshír Márjan".

All that the Páshá, the Shêríf, Shams-ud-dín, and his deputy wrote to me about the dues was merely flattery and deceit. They did nothing for me, as will be seen from what I have written of the treatment I experienced.

CHAPTER III.

JEDDAH is a town on the sea shore. The buildings are distinctly visible from the sea; and in consequence of the houses being six or seven stories high, the town from a distance has an imposing appearance. On entering the city, however, one is struck by the dirty aspect of the streets and their total want of drainage, as well as by their irregular arrangement and the bad construction of the houses.

The day on which I landed in Jeddah was the 14th of the month Sh'abán, A.H. 1280, corresponding to the 24th of January, 1864, of Christ. The evening of that day was the Shab-í-Barát (or Night of Record),[1] and that is an occasion of rejoicing among

[1] The 14th day of the month Sh'abán; when the Mussalmáns make offerings and oblations in the names of deceased relations and ancestors.

the Mussalmáns. Every house was illuminated, either by hanging lanterns or wall-lights, and there was a considerable firing of guns. When I asked the people the reason of this demonstration, some of them replied that it was in honour of the birthday of the Sultan of Turkey; others asserted that it was merely on account of the festival of Shab-í-Barát.

The foundations and walls of the buildings in Mecca are very strong, being composed of either bricks and mortar or stone; but the roofs and floorings are roughly constructed after this fashion:—branches of the date palm are laid cross-wise over the beams and rafters, and over them is spread a layer of earth, so that, if any porous vessel containing water be placed on the floor, the drippings percolate through into the rooms below; or should there be a pan of fire for cooking placed on the floor, the house is in danger of being set on fire. After rain it is common to see grass growing on the roofs. Every house has a kitchen,[1] bath room and other

[1] In India the kitchen and other servants' offices are detached from the house—often several hundred yards off.

offices of masonry, the remainder of the building being composed of mud.

I am speaking now of what I observed myself, but I learned the following particulars (*i.e.* of the manners and customs of the inhabitants) from an old attendant of mine, by name Husen Khán, who accompanied me on the pilgrimage:—every native of India who lands at Jeddah has a dollar or half dollar, according to his condition in life, extorted from him. There is no kindness of disposition among the inhabitants, but they are characterised by a large amount of cruelty and oppression. They consider it a meritorious act to oppress the natives of India—just as a heretic considers it a meritorious act to persecute the true believer. To steal their property or to maltreat them is looked upon as no offence at all.

The manner of buying and selling is after this fashion:—whenever anyone looks at an article admiringly, or asks any question about it, it is immediately handed to him by the seller, and the price demanded; however much he may protest that he was only looking at it, he is not heeded, and if he dispute any further, they spit in his face and insult him. In transactions of this nature the tradesmen are all in collusion, one supporting the other. In short the manners of these people resemble those of the Gonds in India of former days, who were rough mountaineers that lived by rapine and deeds of violence.

The lower orders of Arabs live chiefly on camels' milk, but wine and other intoxicating liquors are commonly drunk in Jeddah, the Turks and others partaking of them.[1] The well-to-do people among the Arabs are fond of good living, and as regards personal appearance are well-looking.

The magistrates and judges are greedy after bribes.

Beyond the city walls, there are some twenty or twenty-five windmills erected; they look like bastions or towers, and have openings in the side, into which are fixed wooden fans; those are turned by the

[1] Mahomed at first permitted to his followers the use of wine in moderation, but afterwards perceiving that total abstinence was the only safeguard against intoxication, he strictly prohibited them from touching what he pronounced to be an "abomination."—(*Vide* "Muir's Life of Mahomed," vol. iii, p. 300.) Hence the Begum's surprise at the unholy practice.

wind, which is constantly blowing off the sea, so that by this means corn can be ground. At the present time, however, the windmills are not at work, and the residents of Jeddah use camels and horses for grinding their corn.[1]

There are about four or five thousand inhabited houses in Jeddah, and the population consists of Arabs, Turks, and Africans. The latter are employed as bargemen and porters; and the traffic on the sea shore consequent on the arrival and departure of ships is very considerable. The Turks and Arabs find occupation as shopkeepers, brokers and soldiers. Good water is extremely scarce in Jeddah: the inhabitants have to bring it from a place about a mile and a half from the city, where between 500 and 1000 pits are dug, in which rain water is collected, and this they use for drinking. After a year or two, the water begins to be brackish, and then the pits are filled up and fresh ones dug.

[1] There are, I believe, no windmills in India (at all events the Begum had never seen one), for their corn and all other kinds of grain are chiefly ground in hand-mills by women.

Confectionery of different sorts is well made in Jeddah, both in the form of sweetmeats and of cakes filled with fruit.

CHAPTER IV.

I NOW proceed with the account of my march from Jeddah: Shêríf Abdúlla (of Mecca) wrote to me as follows:—"It is a long time since we first heard of your intended visit to the holy shrines. Praise be to God that you are on your way! The news has given me much pleasure, and as you will shortly reach Mecca, I have, with reference to the arrangements to be made for your reception, in accordance with your rank, sent to you my brother, together with an interpreter, and they will carry out all your wishes. Be so good as to look upon my relation as your sincere friend; and may you come with perfect ease and comfort to the House of God at Mecca!"

A similar letter came from the Páshá of Mecca with reference to sending his son, Súlímán Beg to meet me.

After this I wrote to my Agent, Abdúl Rahím, saying: "Hire, for the journey to Mecca, eighty camels, at the rate of one Riál[1] each, but let me know if the hire be more of less." The Agent accordingly hired camels for the various stages—viz.: from Jeddah to Mecca, from Mecca to Mina, from Mina to Muzdalifa, from Muzdalifa to 'Arfát, and from thence by the same route back again to Jeddah. One riál proved not to be the fixed rate for every stage, but the hire of the camels varied in price; in some places it was more, in some less. The fact is I had previously written to Shêríf Abdulla and Páshá 'Izzat Ahmed (of Mecca) requesting them to make arrangements for supplying me with camels, mules and horses as far as 'Arfát; and they had replied that "I must negotiate the matter with the Sheikhs of the Bedouins who were the camel drivers; and that this plan was invariably followed by all who made the pilgrimage."

The interpreter Mahomed Húsen, of whom I had made enquiries about the cost of the camels, wrote

[1] A Riál = to twenty-five (25) Kurush is a rix dollar of about the value of four shillings and sixpence.

that "a 'Shagdaf'[1] camel (carrying two people) would be five riáls, of which sum three riáls were for the hire of the camel, and two for the Shagdaf. A Shebrí[2] camel, carrying one person, would be two riáls two kurush, the hire of the animal being two riáls twelve kurush, and the remaining fifteen kurush being for the saddle, &c. Large strong mules were seven riáls each, small mules five riáls; high caste donkeys six riáls, small ones three riáls; for inferior donkeys the price varied according to the quality of the animal ("Jaisá Gadhá waisi kimat:") the highest price for a horse was five riáls."

The only mode of travelling is by riding either camels, horses, donkeys or mules; people of rank, however, only ride on Shagdaf or Shebrí camels.

The donkeys are swift and their paces easy, but their trappings are very indifferent, the saddle consisting of wood covered with leather, and the bridle and stirrups being of rope. Some people ride

[1] A Shagdaf camel carries two square panniers or shagdafs, composed of a frame-work of wood, filled in with rope-work. Each pannier holds one person.

[2] A Shebrí camel carries a kind of square saddle made like a small bed, upon which one person sits.

them astride, and others sit sideways as European ladies ride. The donkeys are fed with beans, grass being scarce, and only have water given to them once in the twenty-four hours. A very large kind of mule, which is called a "Baghlah", sells for a price equal to 200 or 250 rupees (£20 to £25). They are quite as noisy as donkeys, and have the same provender, but get fresh grass and grain when procurable.

At length the price of the camels having been settled by Abdúl Rahím, he took them off to Bakshí Kúdrat Ulla to arrange about their distribution among the different members of the caravan; and about sunset, having mounted our "Shagdaf" camels, we started from Jeddah.

As soon as we had arrived outside the city walls, the Bedouins began to unload the camels, and being asked "why they did so?" they replied,—"When we impress camels for hire, we take half of the number inside the city, and leave the remaining half concealed outside the city walls. The reason of our doing this is, that the chief municipal official would demand his "dastúrí," (perquisite or per-centage profit) on the whole number, and if we refused him that, he would seize the animals and impress them for his own work." Directly, therefore, the camels come outside the city walls, the Bedouins commence unloading them, and the luggage is all thrown into confusion, and frequently some of it is either lost or stolen by them, it is impossible to say which.

Between Jeddah and Haddah (the first stage), I found the "Istikbál"[1] waiting to receive me, and with it were Shêríf Abdulla, brother of the Shêríf of Mecca, and Súlimán Beg, son of the Páshá of Mecca, attended by J'afar Effendi. The latter said to me,—"When the Shêríf comes up and salutes you by saying 'Aselám Alèykyum!' ('Peace be with you!') your Highness must reply—'Alèykyum selám!' ('Upon you be Peace!') Then he will say—'Kèyfhál

[1] "Istikbál," literally "meeting." It is the custom in the East for people of rank to be received at some distance from their destination by a deputation from the house of the host with whom they are to stay. In the case of Royal personages, they are met by some member of the family accompanied by a large retinue; the procession in India on such occasions is very imposing. The British Representatives at the different native Courts in India are received with the like ceremony.

kyùm?' ('How do you do') Your Highness must reply,—'Tâyyib!' ('Very well!')"

After this, the brother of the Shêríf, riding on horseback, came up. The order of the procession was as follows:—About fifty sowars (horse-soldiers) rode behind Shêríf Abdulla, and about the same number of Turkish sowars behind Súlimán Beg, son of the Páshá. The Shêríf was preceded by an Abyssinian seated on horseback, who wore a fur hat which appeared to me to be made of the skin of a shaggy sort of dog; he had two very small kettle-drums in front of him, and rode holding the reins in his mouth and using both hands for beating the drums. When the sun rose, I observed that an umbrella was held over the head of the Shêríf's brother by an Abyssinian riding by his side. The horses were very handsome and well bred, and went along as quietly as if they were kids or lambs tied together; there was no neighing.

Súlimán Beg's escort was similar to that of the Shêríf's brother, only he had but one kettle-drum. They were both accompanied by torch-bearers, and the torches were composed of a particular kind of wood, instead of rags soaked in oil, the ashes of which kept continually falling on the ground as the men moved along. The Shêríf's brother rode by my side for some little distance, but when I told him that the Dowager Begum was coming up behind, he, together with Súliman Beg, left me and went back to meet her.

We reached Haddah at seven o'clock in the morning, and on arrival, I heard the following account from Múnshí Saraj-ud-dín:—"In your Highness' caravan of pilgrims which left Jeddah for the great Mecca, at seven o'clock in the evening of the 15th Sh'abán, was the camel ridden by Her Highness the Kudsíah Begum, and in the middle of the night, while on the road, it was seized by about twenty Bedouins, who began leading it away from the caravan in another direction, when Her Highness called out in a loud voice—'I don't know where those people are taking my camel! They won't listen to, or understand me, and none of my servants are with me. Arí, Arí! (Hullo, there!) Lead my camel along near the Sikandar's camels!' There was with the Kudsíah Begum's camel, a slave whom she had purchased for the pilgrimage, giving him his freedom, and he had joined her at Jeddah; he was clinging round the neck of the camel, and would not let it go, when Búdhú Khán, a Sepoy of the Deorí "Bahádúr" Regiment,[1] one of your Highness' own orderlies, having heard the Kudsíah Begum's voice, ran back, and began to deal such blows with the butt end of his musket at the three or four Bedouins who were leading off the camel, as well as at the ten or twelve others who were surrounding it, that he knocked several of them over; and when they saw that some of their companions were disabled, they left the camel and ran off; Búdhú Khán had been joined, in the meantime, by Ghúlám Húsen and Húsen Baksh, Sepoys of the same regiment, and the three remained with Her Highness as escort."

The Kudsíah Begum herself gave a few more particulars of the occurrence, and said, as she "never imagined the Bedouins who were leading off her camel to be robbers, she entered into conversation with them, under the impression that they were

[1] The "Bahádúr," or "Distinguished" Regiment, raised on the Sikandar Begum's own estate.

escorting her, and told them not to keep her camel by itself, but to lead it along with mine." It was not until she arrived at Haddah that she understood they were robbers.

Kásim Alí, an "employé" of the Bhopál State reported to me as follows:—"When I reached the outer gate of Jeddah, the camel-drivers, that is to say the Bedouins, began turning all the luggage topsy-turvy, and ended with dispatching it in that state. After we had travelled about half a mile, one of the camel-men seized a box full of goods, and a bag containing a bill of exchange and other property belonging to some of the servants of Her Highness (the Dowager Begum). He ran off with these, leaving the camel behind him, the remainder of the caravan having gone on a long way a-head. We, therefore, being quite helpless had no alternative but to return to Jeddah. Arrived there, we procured a donkey from Abdúl Rahím, and with three horse soldiers as escort we again set off, and reached here to-day. On our way we fell in with Mián Idá, who told us to inform your Highness that his camel-men, after having unloaded the camels, had left him where we found him, and that he was perfectly helpless."

On hearing this, I ordered a letter to be written to J'afir Effendi, requesting him to communicate with the Shêríf of Mecca, and to ask him what arrangements could be made for forwarding the goods.

I received a visit at Haddah from the Shêríf's brother and Súlimán Beg, the Páshá's son; but beyond the interchange of a few complimentary speeches we had little conversation.

We remained at Haddah on the 16th of Sh'abán, my agent, Abdúl Rahím, having carelessly forgotten to bring from Jeddah the goats which were to be offered in sacrifice at Mecca. We stayed in the Serai (or travellers' halting place), which consists entirely of "Tatties"[1] made of the dried branches of the date palm. These are erected on the ground, and are under one continuous roof, like military lines, and form four sides of a quadrangle, being partitioned into a number of rooms. In the Tatties which

[1] A Tatti is a kind of screen composed of a framework of wood or bamboo, filled in with dried leaves or grass. They are used in India during the hot weather, inserted in the door-frames, and by being kept constantly wet, moderate the heat of the hot winds.

compose the walls there are openings, but in those of the roof none, that the sun may be effectually kept out—there is a constant breeze flowing through the Tatties. All travellers stay here (in the Serai), and in the compartments intended for people of rank, a mat of date palms is spread, made in the form of a round hookah carpet.

After leaving Haddah we came to Bertoi, near which I was received by an escort of some eighty or ninety infantry and sixty or seventy cavalry, all of whom I dismissed on arrival, telling them I should not proceed on my journey until after I had bathed. There was also a guard of honour posted to receive me, consisting of fifteen or twenty cavalry, and sixty or seventy infantry. The men were drawn up on each side of the road, forming a street. J'afir Effendi came running up to me at this moment, and said: "When these people make their salute, your Highness must say with a loud voice, 'Alèykyum Selám!'" (Peace be upon You!) After the salute was over, some of the guard remained standing where they were, and some accompanied me, and with them were torch-bearers, carrying torches of burning wood.

CHAPTER V.

On Wednesday, the 17th Sh'abán in the year of the Hejra, 1280, corresponding to the 27th January 1864 of Christ, I arrived, in company with my caravan of fellow pilgrims, at the holy Mecca, at seven o'clock in the evening.

I wrote letters to Shêríf Abdulla and Páshá Izzat Ahmed, saying that "on the day of my arrival at Mecca, I was received by a guard of honour consisting of cavalry and infantry; that among these soldiers, I could not distinguish which were in the service of the Shêríf and which in that of the Páshá, and that it was my wish to give a small present (lit. some coffee) to all those who came to receive me at the Istikbál. If agreeable to the Shêríf, I would send it to him, because my people not being acquainted with his, would find it impossible to distribute my gifts."

The Shêríf replied, that, "with regard to a present for the troops at the Istikbál, the Shêríf of Jeddah would give me the necessary information." And Páshá Izzat Ahmed replied, that "to give a present would not be in accordance with the etiquette of the country, and that he hoped I would understand this excuse."

CHAPTER VI.

THE hour of my arrival at Mecca was the 'Ishá (first watch of the night), and the call to evening prayers was sounding from the different mosques. I entered within the holy precincts by the Báb-us-Salám (gate of peace), and, arriving at the house of Abraham, I stood and read the prescribed prayers. After that, I performed the ceremonies of the Toáf-ul-Kudúm,* and of running at the Safá and Marwáh.* It was then my intention to go to the house I had engaged, after I should have offered in sacrifice the animals brought for the purpose, and have accomplished the ceremony of Halak Nisái,* and have also visited the house of Abú-Bakar, the Mutawwaf,[1] where it is

* See Appendices 1 and 2.

[1] Mutawwaf—the guide who conducts pilgrims through the ceremony of the Toáf.

customary for pilgrims to stay. If I should find my own house convenient, I intend remaining there.

In the meantime, however, meeting Molvi 'Abdúl Kai-úm, I asked him to conduct me to my house. He accordingly walked on before me; whereupon one of the four slaves of the Shêríf of Mecca, who had accompanied me from Haddah, ran after him, and, striking him in the face, pushed him against the wall. The Molvi called out in a loud voice, "Look, Madam! one of the Shêríf's slaves is beating me shamefully!" I said to the man, "Bhai! (lit. brother!) why are you beating the Molvi who is one of my people?" He replied, "You are to come to our Shêríf's house, and eat the dinner he has prepared for you." I answered, "The Shêríf has not invited me; I will come back when I have made my offerings." After this, I again proceeded on my way, Molvi 'Abdúl walking before me, when a slave, who was with J'afir Effendi, a very tall, powerful man, drew his sword and began to attack the Molvi. The latter called out to me as before, and I remonstrated with the man who had assaulted him, saying that the Molvi, in obedience to my orders, was showing me the way to my house. The slave replied, "My master the Shêríf's feast, which cost him 5000 rupees, is all getting spoilt, and his money is being wasted!" J'afir Effendi then said, "Your Highness had better go to the Shêríf's, otherwise he will be very angry, and his anger is certainly not pleasant." On hearing this, I bent my steps to the Shêríf's house, and, arriving there, I found his brother, Abdullah, waiting for me, who, after having made a "salám," and inquired how I was, took his leave. I made the prescribed offerings at his door, and performed the ceremony of Halak Nisái. On entering the house, I found a room in which a handsomely embroidered velvet carpet was spread, and in front of the room, on the top of an open portico, dinner was laid upon a table-cloth. The repast consisted of about five hundred specimens of Arabian cookery, some of the dishes savoury, some sweet. They said to me, "Eat your dinner." I excused myself by replying that I had had no invitation. J'afir Effendi said to me, "If you do not eat, the Shêríf will be very displeased, and it would never do to offend him." Then, stooping down, he whispered in my ear, "When the Shêríf is angry with people, he orders his head slaves to shoot them in the night, and *you* have to perform the Toáf;[1] on this account, then, do not make the Shêríf angry." After this, I said nothing more, but sat down and began to eat. The dew had fallen upon the food, making it as cold as ice, so that nothing had any flavour. J'afir Effendi and some Turks attended upon me at the meal. After it was over, night having set in, we passed it there.

When we got up in the morning, I saw that a carpet, richly embroidered with gold, had been laid down, and, thinking that from our eating Pán[2] upon it, it might be spoiled, I caused it to be folded up and given to J'afir Effendi, desiring him to send it to the Shêríf, but I do not know whether or not he told the latter for what reason I had given this order.

In the meantime, the Turkish attendants brought in some twenty or twenty-five trays, and J'afir

[1] Which ceremony would entail the necessity of the Begum going out in the dark.

[2] The spices and beetul nut eaten continually by the natives of India.

Effendi came with them. He said, "The Shêríf has sent this repast." I replied, "I partook of his dinner last night, why has he sent me more this morning? It is not customary to feast a guest after the first day." He said—"It is our custom in this country to send travellers meals twice a day for three days." I replied,—"How can I partake of this repast, without having been informed regarding it, and without any invitation from the Shêríf?" He said,—"You *must* keep it; it is impossible for you to return it, for by so doing you would make the Shêríf very angry." To this I said,—"If, according to the entiquette of this country, the Shêríf intends feasting me for three days, let him do so when the ship arrives with all my retinue. I arrived here with only twenty or twenty-five people in my suite, and the Shêríf has sent me enough food for one or two hundred people. Among whom can I distribute it? The Shêríf's entertainment is being wasted." The Turks who brought the breakfast became very angry, and said,—"You are disobeying the Shêríf's order, and treating him with disrespect." I replied,—"I am only speaking of a matter of custom and etiquette, and you accuse me of want of politeness, and of disrespect to the Shêríf. Well, set down the breakfast, but do not bring any more food to-night." As soon as I had said this, the dishes were put down, and divided among my people; I, also, ate a little. In the evening, the Turks brought the same supply of food again, whereupon I told them that part of the breakfast was still lying untouched, and that there were no people to divide this meal among, therefore they had better take it away. On hearing this, a Turk became very angry, and said, Heaven knows what, in his own language, and remained talking a long time. Judging from his manner that he was very indignant, I allowed my people to take a portion of the dinner, and caused the remainder of the trays to be returned.

In the meantime, the Dowager Begum and Nawáb Faujdár Mahomed Khán arrived from the house where they were staying, and put up in the same house with me; and the Turks having taken away the dinner, did not return.

After we had said our prayers and performed the Toáf, we all went to bed. Next morning, at about seven o'clock, some twenty or twenty-five Turks, armed and dressed in uniform, arrived and rushed into the house in an excited way; they seized the Shêríf's embroidered carpet, which was lying folded up, and then pulled the mat, upon which two girl attendants of mine were sitting, from under them, and threw it away, after having beaten the girls with sticks.

After this, proceeding to the apartments of Mián Faujdár Mahomed Khán, they entered the kitchen where the cooking was going on, threw water over the stoves, and put out the fire; they then broke all the earthern water vessels and spilt the water. One of the Turks addressing the Nawáb said: "You must not stay in the Shêríf's house—you have been speaking ill of him." The Nawáb replied: "Speak the truth now! In whose presence have I said anything against him?"

A Turk now came up to where I was, and sitting down in a most familiar and disrespectful way in my presence, began talking in Arabic in an angry tone. My Agent Hájí Húsen, who was sitting with me at the time, explained to me that the man said: "This woman is not worthy of the honour of sitting on this carpet; she has disobeyed the Shêríf's orders." To this I made no reply; but I ordered a letter to be written to Háfiz Mahomed Húsen Khán, detailing the exact state of the case in the matter of the carpet, and the anger of the Turks, and I desired him to go to the Shêríf and ask: "Why we, sojourning as travellers, had been rebuked after this fashion? If it were not agreeable to him that I should remain in his private house, he had only to signify his pleasure, and in compliance with His Excellency's orders, I should vacate it. For this reason, that we were only travellers, staying here at his will, as long as we should be detained in performing the ceremonies connected with the pilgrimage of Islám. It would be well, therefore, that His Excellency should adopt the plan I had pursued in appointing an agent for transacting business with him, and on his part depute some intelligent and capable secretary to communicate with me, who should be able to explain all directions of the Shêríf on any matter, be it great or small, that I might be enabled to carry them out. That I wished him to put a stop entirely to the Turks and Arabs intruding upon me, because

I neither understood their language nor they mine; and Heaven only knew what from this mutual misunderstanding, they might not report to the Shêríf, who, owing to their misrepresentations, might be displeased without the slightest cause."

CHAPTER VII.

AFTER having heard this, the Shêríf wrote to me, through Shêríf Háshím, as follows: "The duty of providing resting-places for the nobles who visit this city, devolves upon us Shêrífs, as well as the care of securing lodgings for the whole company of the Faithful and followers of Islám. Consequently, every person of rank entitled to consideration at our hands, receives the due amount of dignity and respect his position should command. We, therefore, having regard to your Highness' rank and the honour pertaining thereto, as well as to the friendship of long standing existing between your Highness' mother and my father, on hearing of your arrival from Molví Yákúb, were the more anxious to show every respect to your Highness, and in accordance with the custom of this country, we prepared a house provided with every comfort, for your reception. Your Highness' mother, after having come to the very door of the house, went off to one that she had hired, in spite of every persuasion to the contrary. I took no notice, however, of this unpleasant occurrence. I heard afterwards that your Highness was not pleased with the entertainment provided, and that you had removed from the lower rooms which I had had carpeted, to the upper rooms, where you had caused your own carpet to be laid down. I understood from this that your Highness did not choose to sit on my carpet. I had every desire to secure your Highness' comfort, and therefore I had asked you for your own convenience sake to occupy the lower rooms, being under the impression that Indian people preferred the ground floor.

I have now laid before you for your Highness' satisfaction a statement of the circumstances which occasioned you annoyance."

In reply to this, I caused a letter to be written to Háfiz Mahomed Khán, the Naib Bakshí, in which I said: "I desire to acknowledge with thanks the respect and politeness shown by the Shêríf to us travellers, but the fact of the matter is this: that, whatever may be the etiquette regarding the reception of strangers, no explanation thereof was given to me, either at first by the Shêríf's brother, or by any of his dependents, whether officers or servants; neither did I ever receive a visit from Molví Yákúb, nor was there any interchange of politeness between us. The Dowager Begum, after leaving Bertoi, proceeded in advance of me, and I know nothing about her having gone to His Excellency's house and having left it again; but this much I do know, that Her Highness is suffering from pain in her back, and could not occupy an upper-storied house in consequence. Moreover, it is contrary to the custom of our country that a daughter, after her marriage, should with her suite, reside in the same house with her father and mother. I know nothing of any persuasions that were used to induce the Begum to remain."

I also wrote regarding the affair of Molví 'Abdúl Kai-úm and the violence of the Shêríf's slaves towards him; also of my intention of returning to the house prepared for me by the Shêríf, after I should have gone to the one I had engaged, and I related the circumstances of the entertainment which had been served to me without any previous intimation from the Shêríf. To this I added: "We, being Afgháns, pay great respect and reverence to the descendants of Fatima, so much so that from any Syed[1] who may be in the cavalry or infantry, no chief takes a Nazar.[2] Now the Shêríf is our Chief, as well as Lord of the whole world, and on account of his exalted dignity, I caused the very beautiful carpet which he had had laid down for me in the house prepared for my reception, to be folded up, in case that from the coming and going of people, it should be injured in any way. I also told J'afir Effendi that I had fixed upon a residence for my own occupation, which, however, in consequence of its being very high was not altogether convenient. Notwithstanding this drawback, I only consider my one object, which is to perform the pilgrimage, and

[1] The Syeds are descendants of Ali, who married Fatima, Mahomed's daughter.

[2] A Nazar is an offering from an inferior to a superior.

to cement the friendship existing between the Shêríf's family and my own. For the latter reason, I am most anxious to avoid displeasing him in any respect, and to give no grounds to his people for setting him against me. It is advisable, therefore, as long as I shall remain in Mecca, that the Shêríf and I should mutually inform each other beforehand of the customs of our respective countries, and that we should severally appoint officers, to see that the proper entiquette is observed between us. By this means all occasions of offence will be avoided. I have heard that a sister of the Shêríf was living in the house he placed at my disposal, and that she removed into another for my accommodation. I think she cannot experience the same amount of comfort in a house that is not her own, and as going up-and-down-stairs is fatiguing to me, I will with the Shêríf's kind permission occupy the house I have engaged, thereby enabling his sister to return to her own house. I shall therefore await the expression of the Shêríf's wishes."

To this Shêríf Abdulla replied: "In accordance with the custom of this Court, and to show my friendship for you, I sent my brother to receive you with the Istikbál; it is both right and proper that the remaining hospitable observances (which consist of an entertainment lasting three days) should be carried out; and as my servants knew that the custom was both an established and invariable one, they thought it superfluous to give you any notice, either of the entertainment or with regard to your staying in my house. This will account for your having heard nothing of the matter. I now, being acquainted with the custom of your country, find that I acted contrary to your etiquette, however, it was done unintentionally, so let bygones be bygones. Now, our friendship is established on a sure basis. It is no trouble to me to render you every assistance in my power; and, although I do not see the necessity for informing you beforehand, every transaction between us shall be to our mutual satisfaction, in accordance with the request contained in your letter. The house is entirely at your disposal, and by occupying it you have inconvenienced no one, neither is any return expected for it; still, if you consider that it is not adapted to you, you must decide as you think best."

On receiving this I wrote to the Deputy Commander-in-Chief (Naib Bakshi) and told him to go to the Shêríf and say from me "that his courteous reply had given me much pleasure; that adjoining the house I had rented there were five other houses, not government buildings, which I should be obliged by his obtaining for me, in order that privacy might be insured to me during my stay for the period of Ramzán,[1] and that I would send the rent to him."

The Naib Bakshí wrote in answer, that the Shêríf had ordered the chief magistrate of the city to purchase the five buildings, and make them over to me, and that he had told him verbally, if I did not like to remain in his house, he would not be hurt or annoyed at my leaving it; for he only desired my comfort, and wherever I could be most comfortable, there I had better remain. He added,

[1] Ramzán is a Mahomedan fast observed with great strictness during the month called by its name. From the appearance of the first streak of light on the horizon, until the stars are clearly seen at eventide not a particle of food or a drop of water is allowed to be taken.

"The pilgrimage is a sacred duty, but it is incumbent on every one performing it to provide himself with a house suitable to his rank in life. I do not say that the Begum need necessarily remain in my house, but it is proper that she should select one adapted to the occupation of a personage of her great name and exalted dignity."

Notwithstanding the Shêríf's persistent refusal to take any rent, he accepted it willingly enough when the time came for me to leave.

At length the chief magistrate, through the medium of my prime minister, rented to me two buildings; one, a college, for my own occupation, and the other a private mansion for the accommodation of the pilgrims in my suite.

When I went to the Shrine at 'Arfát, at the first stage, Mina, I engaged three buildings for my stay of three days, and found when I had to pay for them that a year's rent was demanded; the rule being that if one remained a day only, one had to pay a year's rent.

I now wrote again, both to the Shêríf and Páshá of Mecca, saying that, "As long as I should remain there, I should apply to them in every case of difficulty, Providence having made them Lords of the country; and for this reason I had appointed my Naib Bakshí and Captain Mittú Khán to wait upon them on all occasions, that they might be fully informed by them regarding all matters of etiquette, and that every chance of misunderstanding might be avoided, for that I, not being acquainted with Arabic, was unable to give directions in that language."

The Shêríf replied, "What your Highness writes is very true, and I have appointed on my part, Háshím-Bin-Shêríf, to transact my business with you during the whole of your Highness' stay. And for your agents, I accept the Naib Bakshí and Captain Mittú Khán. Mahomed Húsen, the interpreter, will act under their orders."

CHAPTER VIII.

THE City of Mecca the Exalted is very wild and desolate-looking, and is surrounded by lofty hills, quite destitute of trees. These hills extend, I am told, to a distance of four or five marches on all sides of Mecca; and I found on the 'Amrah road that this was the case. The road runs between the hills, being in some places so narrow as to admit of only three or four camels going abreast, and in others wide enough for five or ten.

The months of February and March were cool during my stay in Mecca (whereas the weather at that season in India is hot); however, the people told me they had not had such cold weather for the time of year for eighteen or nineteen years, but that the heat had been intense (lit., "it had rained fire"). During my visit we had cloudy weather about every two days, alternately with warm weather for two days, and occasionally it rained for an hour to two; once, too, we had hail for a day or so.

There was a great deal of severe sickness, and the inhabitants of Mecca suffered considerably. Nine people in my suite were attacked with various complaints, such as dysentery, fever, and tumours in the leg. On the pilgrimage, I lost eight altogether, four of whom died on board ship and four at Mecca and Jeddah. In the caravan that separated from me and went to Medina, a great many people died, some on land and some on board ship. Two persons also disappeared out of my suite, and were never found again: one was a woman whom we lost on the pilgrimage, and the other a water-carrier who went to Medina. I do not know what became of them.

In the country round Mecca, there are neither lakes, rivers, nor streams, there are only springs, and in these no travellers are allowed to bathe without payment. People of the poorer classes are beaten and driven away from them, sentries belonging to the Shêríf and Páshá being posted over them. The water is sold at the rate of half a kurush a skin full. A chief, or person of rank, who is acquainted with the Shêríf and Páshá, can obtain a sufficient supply of water for the needs of his establishment. I had permission to receive as much as I wanted. There are magnificent baths in the city, those for men being separate from the women's.

The plan on which dwelling-houses are built is very objectionable, the sitting and sleeping apartments being close to the kitchen[1] and other domestic offices, so that one is annoyed in the sitting-rooms by smoke from the kitchen. Notwithstanding this drawback, the furniture of the rooms, as regards carpets and divans is excellent; but the arrangements for lighting them are bad, the chandeliers and wall lamps being few in number. The houses are amply provided with crockery and vessels of brass and copper, and are built on the hills in the same way as they are at Raisen[2]—buildings

[1] As I have before remarked, the kitchen and servants' offices in India are not under the same roof with the house, but are generally separated by a distance of some hundred yards.

[2] Raisen is a town in the Begum's territory of Bhopal.

cover the hill from the foot to the summit. The houses are without courtyards, and are built in flats or stories, capable of being added to at pleasure; no house had fewer than three stories, nor any more than seven. Some of them have door-frames, and some are without them; those that have door-frames have no doors, and where the latter are used there are neither chains nor hasps, locks nor bolts, not even hinges, the doors being fastened with a sort of wooden lock made in the shape of a cross, such as Christians wear round their necks. Houses belonging to people of the upper class have open vestibules of masonry in front, those that are used for dining in are generally without roofs, on account of the heat.

I made enquiries respecting the price of building materials, and found that the tariff was as follows:-

Lime (in Mecca itself)

12 measures, or

one chest . . . 4 kurush[1]

Bricks, 1st quality, per

1000 . . . 2 riáls[2] 10 kurush

[1] A kurush is 1/25 of a riál.

[2] A riál (rix dollar) is worth about 2s. 6d.

Do. 2nd quality, per
1000 . . . 1 riál 5 kurush

Do. 3rd quality, per
1000 . . . 1 riál

Stones, 1st quality, per
1000 . . . 4 riáls

Do. 2nd quality, per
1000 . . . 2 riáls

Timber for beams, from 1 rupee[1] 8 annas each to 1 rupee 4 annas 3 pie.[2]

Do. for rafters, from 5 to 6 kurush each.

The sanitary arrangements of the city are very much as I have described them to be at Jeddah, the streets being dirty and ill-drained; in some places they are broad, in others narrow.

The population is considerable, there being about 20,000 houses.

There is a fort in Mecca mounted with guns, but the guns are dirty and the ammunition is bad. The Turks are very dirty in their habits, and gross livers; I

[1] I rupee 8 annas equal to 3s.

[2] I rupee 4 annas 3 pie equal to about 2s. 6¼d.

do not know whether they are well set up or not when in uniform or at drill, but in their houses they are very dirty and untidy in their dress.

Camels are bred very extensively; cows, bullocks, goats, and sheep are perhaps about as plentiful as they are in India, but there are more of the thick-tailed sheep. There are no buffaloes. The horses are very superior and costly, but their trappings are not so, nor do the people ride well. I have heard that the Turks do, however.

Donkeys, mules, dogs, cats, flies, mosquitoes, &c., abound, also kites; but I saw neither common nor musk rats.

We saw on the hill on the road to 'Amrah a great many locusts (which do considerable injury to the crops); they were in such numbers, that one could not see the ground for them. The Bedouins gather them in baskets and use them for food.

There is a great consumption of meat, tea, and ghee,[1] which latter is made from the milk of the cow and the thick-tailed sheep.

[1] Clarified butter.

In Mecca the people can neither sing nor dance, but most of the women whistle, clapping their hands and snapping their fingers as an accompaniment. On the occasion of weddings,[1] ladies sing comic songs and dance, but they do both so badly, that one has not the slightest pleasure in hearing or seeing them, but is rather disgusted than otherwise.

Amateurs of the kind of music we have in India, practise it stealthily in their houses.

When the Shêríf goes out, he is accompanied by people playing kettle-drums. In the Turkish regiments they use large drums, but do not play upon them in the English fashion.

No one but Mussulmans are allowed to practise their religious rites publicly.

There are Indian and Turkish medical practitioners in Mecca, and also dispensaries, in which the medical systems of their respective countries are followed.

The etiquette of paying and receiving visits is the same as in India, but most people only exchange

[1] It is not customary in India for ladies either to sing or dance.

them from self-interested motives; wealthy persons seeking for introductions with the expectation of making money thereby,—there is no interchange of sincerity and friendship. Every one is well off, but they are all miserly and covetous; it is no disgrace to any one to beg; high and low, young men and old, women, boys and girls of all grades, are more or less beggars. Give them what you will, they are never satisfied. Even when work-people are paid for their labour, they do nothing satisfactorily, and demand their pay before their work is complete. The employers also, on their part, cheat as much as they can.

The custom of taking perquisites prevails to such an extent among all classes, that if one only wants to hire a donkey for the pilgrimage, one has to employ an agent, and this man gets a commission from the owner of the animal upon the hire of it, the sum of a kurush or half kurush. On all occasions of buying and selling, the same custom prevails. It is usual to demand the price of an article the moment it is sold; one is not trusted for an instant.

It seemed to me that begging was held to be as

honourable as working; and when travellers take their departure (from Mecca), they are beseiged by nobles as well as plebeians who clamour obstinately and violently for "bukhsheesh."

Almost all the bad characters that have been driven out of India, may be found in Mecca.

Imports from every part of the world are procurable, but the price of everything is dear.

Women frequently contract as many as ten marriages, and those who have only been married twice are few in number. If a woman sees her husband growing old, or if she happens to admire any one else, she goes to the Shêríf, and after having settled the matter with him, she puts away her husband, and takes to herself another, who is perhaps young, good-looking, and rich. In this way a marriage seldom lasts more than a year or two.

The inhabitants of the Desert, who are Bedouins, understand nothing about cooking, but eat uncooked food, also such things as honey, dates and ghee, with avidity.

The inhabitants of the city wear clothes, but those of the desert in place of clothes, content themselves with skins and blankets. Some of the Bedouins wear a long kind of shirt, without any waist-belt or girdle. Most of them leave their heads uncovered, but some wear a rope made of date-palm fibre, or such like material, bound round their head.

The people who reside in the cities know something of religion, but those who inhabit the mountainous regions are totally ignorant of it.

Arabic is the language used in conversation, but pure Arabic is only spoken by a few,—the city people do not speak it.

The vendors of various goods carry on business in this way: if they ask a rupee for any article, and the intending purchaser offers half that sum for it, the salesman throws dirt at his customer, and spits in his face; and when he takes the price of an article either in silver or copper, if it be a small sum, he puts it into his mouth instead of using a purse or bag.

There is no salt used in cooking in this part of the world, but besides pickles and chutneys, they make sweet dishes without number.

There are more inhabitants of Delhi in Mecca

than of any other place. Fermented liquors are sold, but not openly, and the Turks and natives of India drink them.

The military and other subjects of the Sultan of Turkey who come on the pilgrimage to Mecca are much feared by the inhabitants of the illustrious city, and consequently have less trouble there than the pilgrims who come from India.

After prayer-time and the ceremony of Toáf, there is a great noise in the sacred precincts.

There is no fixed tariff in the bazaar; every shop has its own price,—they get what they can.

Everybody, whether of high rank or low, goes on foot.

Cheating and lying prevail to a great extent; and the children are very disorderly and noisy. There are no colleges or schools for affording them instruction, and the men and women are a worthless set of people.

There is no one particular dress worn; Arabs and others all wear the costume of their respective countries.

I noticed on the hill Jabal Núr, which I visited, small pebbles of all colours; some red, some green, some golden. The people who come from Java to the pilgrimage are said to extract gold from them.

The jungle round Mina is very dense and wild; and I heard that many poisonous reptiles, such as scorpions, snakes, &c., are found there.

CHAPTER IX.

I LEARNT the following anecdotes from Akbar Khán, a servant of the State of Bhopál, who was one of my suite on the pilgrimage:—

"I went to bathe in the tank, which is small, and the only one in Mecca, and found there a great many men and women assembled to bathe; among them were a Bedouin and a native of India. The Bedouin asked the latter for his soap, but he would not give it, whereupon the Bedouin instantly struck at him on the shoulder with his knife, but the people protected him from further violence, and the Bedouin got out of the way. He then came to the place where I was washing my clothes, and begged of me in the same way. Having seen what he had just done, I refused his request, and violent language followed; after which the Bedouin, having filled a bucket with water, began to help me wash my clothes, and as soon as I had finished washing them, I gave him the remainder of my soap.

"An Egyptian went into a baker's shop, and asked the price of the bread. When the baker told him, the Egyptian wanted him to take less, but the baker seized a broom and struck the man in the face, giving him at the same time plenty of abuse, and saying at last something so violent, that the Egyptian began pelting him with stones, and threw down all the contents of his shop on the ground.

"Occurrences such as these are constantly happening, and business transactions are carried on in this fashion between the lower orders and travellers. No one interferes in the matter."

The buying and selling of male and female slaves of all races take place in the slave market. There are a great many Africans sold, and they are exposed for sale on a "Dakkah" (*i.e.* a level spot), where they are all collected together; and purchasers having selected them and paid the price, on obtaining a receipt, take them away from there. Georgian men and women are also sold; these people come in the caravans to the pilgrimage, and the inhabitants of Mecca buy them and sell them again to the pilgrims. In this way the sale lasts for two days every year. Some of the women are taken in marriage, and after that, on being sold again, they receive from their masters a divorce, and are sold in their houses, that is to say, they are sent to the purchaser from their master's house on receipt of payment, and are not exposed for sale on the "Dakkah." They are only married when purchased for the first time. The women who have children are allowed to sit down in their masters' presence; but with this exception, all women are compelled to stand in an attitude of respect. This is the custom prevailing among the upper classes. The nobles also purchase Africans and Georgians and send them to the shrines in the capacity of servants, for performing such duties as sweeping, lighting the lamps, &c.; some of them receive a year's supply of food and other necessaries at a time. When the poorer people buy slaves, they keep them for themselves, and change them every year, as one would replace old things by new; but the women who have children are not sold. The

Africans are dealt with in the same way, and the poorer classes purchase them for performing menial kind of work in their own houses, such as sweeping, lighting the lamps, washing clothes, fetching water, carrying burdens, serving at meals, and conveying goods from one shop to another. These have clothes for the year, and food twice a day given to them. Some of the female slaves are let out by their masters for daily labour, and the latter take their day's hire. When they behave badly, they are sold; but as a rule, the slaves make very faithful servants; after working at drawing water the whole day, they put their wages into the hands of their masters, and receive only two loaves of bread for themselves.

During the season of Ramzán,[1] there is a great deal of reciting litanies at night: one cannot catch, however, a word of what is said, it sounds like a confused noise. At the call to prayers, they use a sort

[1] Ramzán is the ninth Mahomedan month, during which a strict fast is observed; neither eating nor drinking is allowed between the morning dawn and the appearance of the stars at night. Prayers offered up on the 19th, 21st, and 23rd days are supposed to be peculiarly efficacious.

of chanting (called by the Persians Ilhán) and change the key from a high to a low one. There are five calls to prayer made in the same way as in India, but one at night time, more than in India. There is one form of thanksgiving in the evening from four o'clock till sunset, *i.e.*, "God, He is great; God, He is great. There is no god but God, and He is great. Praise be to God!" There is one form of prayer in the early morning, in which many verses from the venerable Korán are read on the subject of the Oneness, the Majesty and the Glory of the All Merciful God, and others also relating to the Prophet of God—on whom rest mercy and peace!—and to the four great friends.[1] This is said at dawn, and on this occasion the chanting is so complicated, that one cannot comprehend a word of it. They read with a full, clear voice.

[1] Mahomed, Ali, Omar, and Abubakr.

CHAPTER X.

WHEN I was settled in Mecca, the Fakírs[1] used to assemble in such crowds before my doors that not only our meals, but our devotions were greatly interrupted. This was caused by the lavish liberality of Her Highness the Dowager Begum, and to put a stop to the inconvenience, I wrote to the Naib Bakhshí and desired him to direct the Sentries and Sowárs (who were posted over the house lent me by the Shêríf, and over the buildings rented by me) to inform me when the crowd of Fakírs at the doors became excessive, that I might send for some of the Turks belonging to the Shêríf to drive them away. If there were only one or two Fakírs, the Sepoy was to order them off, and if any Turks remained

[1] Religious mendicants.

at the doors, I was to be informed of it.

After arrangements had been made about the Fakírs, the Turks and Arabs commenced the same system of annoyance: they went about whenever and wherever they pleased; neither sitting nor sleeping apartments were sacred to them, no one knew when they might be expected, for they came when they pleased, but more especially at meal times, and without any invitation they would remain and sit down to eat with us. Some of them, moreover, behaved in the same way towards the soldiers of our escort, and when the men were cooking their food out of doors, if a Bedouin chanced to come up leading his camel, or engaged in any other occupation, he would join whoever might happen to be eating his dinner, and commence partaking of it; nay, he would even seize the food from a man and appropriate the whole of it with perfect complacency. Then, having returned thanks, and given his blessing to the man whose food he had devoured, he would go away, utterly indifferent to the hunger of the individual whose dinner he had appropriated without permission.

I wrote to the Naib Bakshí, and told him that not even the upper story rooms where we slept, were safe from intrusion; and I directed him to station one or two of my own people near the door of the room I had assigned to him as a sleeping apartment, with instructions to admit no one without my orders, excepting the wife of J'afir Effendi, the sister of Nawáb Nazír-ud-Daulah Umráo Dúlah Báki Mahomed Khán,[1] and any other ladies who spoke Hindustani.

[1] The husband of the Sikandar Begum's daughter.

CHAPTER XI.

I WAS now settled in Mecca, and began to be occupied with my religious exercises.

After Her Highness the Nawáb Dowager Begum had presented to the Shêríf, the Páshá and Shebí Sáhib[1] the gifts she had brought for them from Bhopál, the fame of her liberality and great riches spread to such an extent throughout the whole city of Mecca, that she was completely mobbed by Fakírs, and the possibility of her performing the Toáf was entirely put an end to. I felt perfectly helpless, and began to question the utility of having gone to Mecca for devotional ends. I accordingly requested the Shêríf and Páshá to make over to me some of their Turks, to form part of my suite when

[1] The Keeper of the keys of the holy places.

I made the Toáf, and so protect me from the violence of the Fakírs. The Shêríf, in compliance, ordered four Turks to attend me when performing the Toáf. They did this, and when they had safely escorted me home, they were going away after having made their "salám," but I judged from their demeanour that they expected a present, although they had not asked for one. I consequently ordered a present of eight annas[1] to be given to each man daily. They took it without any compunction, and seemed in no fear of punishment at the result.

We were in the habit of wearing Turkish veils[2] when going out on the Toáf and other expeditions, and the inhabitants of Mecca enquired of my people "which among those women was the Sikandar Begum of Bhopál?" Some of them were foolish enough to point me out, so to avoid a repetition of the annoyance, I issued an order to all my suite, forbidding them, on pain of dismissal from my

[1] One shilling.

[2] The Begum of Bhopál and the ladies of her family do not ordinarily cover their faces as is customary among Mussulman women.

service, to cause me to be recognized, either in doors or out of doors, by any one, be they inhabitants of Mecca, or strangers.

This point being settled, I discovered that some worthless and disreputable people among my dependants had commenced a system of making requests in my name to the Shêríf and Páshá. I, of course, prohibited this, and caused a copy of my orders on the subject to be sent to both those gentlemen, together with a letter to the following effect:—"Any communication you may have to make to me should come either through the Naib Bakshí, Captain Mittú Khan, or the interpreter, Mahomed Húsen; and if any person in my suite besides them make a request in my name, they are not to be attended to."

The substance of my orders was to the effect that I forbade all my people on pain of dismissal from my service, to go to their Excellencies on any pretext whatever.

CHAPTER XII.

HAVING learnt from my Prime Minister that a person named Sheikh Ahmed Effendi, a Dághastáni,[1] was a good Turkish scholar, I formed a project, at the suggestion of my Minister, of having the venerable Korán translated into Turkish, in order that those Turks who were unable to understand it in the original, might become acquainted with it by this means. I accordingly spoke to the Dághastání on the subject, and he agreed to translate it. I then wrote to the Shêríf and Páshá, informing them of my desire that the Holy Word might be translated, in order that the Turkish people might read it, and be

[1] A Dághastání is a guide to the shrines and other celebrated spots visited by the pilgrims.

profited thereby. The Páshá wrote in reply, that a translation of the Korán itself was not allowed; that there were translations of what the commentators had written upon it, and that my informant, whoever it might have been, had misled me on the subject. "Learned people," (he added), "who are versed in Arabic, are able to peruse the commentaries in that language; and with regard to the lower orders, therc are numerous interpretations of the Korán in Turkish—for instance, that well-known and trustworthy one called 'Tibyán', and most likely this is to be had in Mecca."

The Páshá's ideas seemed to me to be adverse to the weal of the common people, and I therefore directed the Dághastání to make a translation into Turkish of the Word of God, and to send it to me.

I now wrote to Syed Abú Bakar, the Mutawaf,[1] and said that if he could procure for me all the "Ghiláfs," (hangings or coverings) of the holy shrines in Mecca, I should esteem it a great favour and be

[1] The guide who conducts the pilgrims to perform the Toáf.

extremely gratified,[1] and would willingly pay whatever price might be asked for them.

The Páshá himself wrote to me on the subject and said: "When the caravan of pilgrims returns to Mecca from 'Arfat, the price of the Ghiláfs can be determined on. The Sultan of Turkey does not send new coverings for the interior of the holy places every year, and it is impossible to fix a price for the same. I will, on receiving the Ghiláfs, communicate with your Highness, through Syed Abú Bakr, the Most High God being willing. The exterior coverings are taken away every year by an inhabitant of Mecca, and having procured them at the prescribed rate from him, I will send them to you. The Nawáb Kudsíah Begum has also written to

[1] Of the Ghiláfs here alluded to, I learnt the following particulars from the Minister of Bhopál, after the death of the Sikandar Begum:—They are coverings for the domes and other portions of the holy places at Mecca. Those that are used for the exterior hangings, are of a black material, with sentences from the Korán embroidered on them in raised letters,—and these are renewed every year, the old ones being the perquisite of Shebí Sahib (keeper of the keys of the sanctuary.) The hangings that are used for the interior are of red silk, with raised letters in white; these are only changed on the occasion of the death of the Sultan of Turkey, and the old ones go to Shebí Sahib.

me regarding the price of the curtains of the holy places, and I have to inform her that those curtains sell for 600 or 700 riáls. The curtains at the doors, and the screens on the four sides which are covered with gold leaf, go to the Páshá and Shebí Sahib, and the whole cost of the same is from 1300 to 1400 riáls.[1] Anything in excess of this price, would be considered in the light of a present, and such a gift would not be without its reward."

The Naib Bakshí also wrote to say that the Shêríf had promised to send the curtains, but that the price I had paid for them was too small, and that we must send him something more. The curtain that surrounds the centre of the shrine fetches, when sold, as much as between 2800 and 3000 riáls.[2] The fact of the matter is, that after I returned to Bhopál, the Páshá neither sent the curtains nor returned the money he had received[3] for them. The

[1] Upwards of £300.

[2] About £600.

[3] The exterior hangings of the shrines arrived at Bombay just as the Sikandar Begum died in November, 1868, and a guard was sent from Bhopál to receive the much-valued relics with all due honour, and escort them to Bhopál.

second request of the Shêríf for more money I did not comply with, and the consequence is, that a correspondence between us is still going on, through the medium of the Consul of Jeddah.

Captain Mittú Khan wrote to inform me he had heard from the Shêríf, in reply to two letters of mine, that the interior coverings of the holy shrines are only renewed on the accession to the throne of a new Sultan of Turkey.

I wrote to Páshá Izzat Ahmed informing him that I was writing two letters to Pásha Sarkash of Medina, on the subject of the coverings, both of the interior and exterior of the shrine of the Holy Prophet,[1] and that I should esteem it a favour on his part, if he would forward the reply of the Páshá to me. I enclosed him copies of the two letters, in order that he might have a clear understanding of the matter.

The Páshá wrote in reply: "The coverings of the tomb of the Intercessor for Sinners (*i.e.* Mahomed), unlike those of the Temple of the Lord of the

[1] At Medina.

Universe (*i.e.* God), are not for both exterior and interior, but consist of a single hanging, and that is not changed every year, but at considerably long intervals; and it is preserved as a relic with the regalia of the Empire of Turkey. A small portion of it, however, is kept back, for distribution among certain chief personal attendants on the Páshá of Medina, and is divided among them, in accordance with an ancient custom. This covering of the tomb of the Glory of all existence was changed last year by the Sultan, and it would not be possible to obtain more than a very small portion of the curtain. I will, however, write myself to-day or to-morrow, to the Páshá of Medina regarding it, and ask for as much of it as can be procured."

Notwithstanding this, I returned to Bhopál without any of the curtain, and the Páshá has never sent it to me.

Round the holy places at Mecca there is a series of buildings (or cloisters) built against the outer wall of the Mosque itself, known by the name of the "Madrassah," (*lit.* College), and these are rented by the pilgrims, for the purpose of affording to the old and infirm, to invalids and women (which latter are forbidden to show themselves in public) an opportunity of their joining in the prayers at the prescribed hours; and it is accounted the same as saying prayers in the shrine itself. After the prayers are over and the crowd diminishes, they go within the holy places and perform the ceremony of Toáf only.

Súlimán Beg, son of Páshá Izzat Ahmed came to pay me a visit, and as he was only able to speak Turkish, Sheikh J'afir Effendi acted as interpreter between us. After he arrived there was some delay on my part before I could receive him, and I excused myself by saying: "As Friday is the day for the performance of religious observances, I had undressed myself for the prescribed ablutions, and was therefore late in making my appearance, and I hoped he would forgive me."

Súlimán Beg replied: "I fear I have inconvenienced you." I said: "It is the custom in our country, when people of rank visit each other, to give notice of one's coming two hours beforehand, in order that the people of the house, leaving all other occupations, may be ready for the visit." He replied: "I now understand your custom." After this I enquired of him the rate of pay of the Turkish servants, and he said: "The pay they receive is twenty kurush, that is three and a half rupees a month, but besides this they have their food, and an allowance of soap for washing their clothes, also livery, and money for tea, &c. When the whole amount is reckoned together in the office, it comes to about twenty-one rupees."

I then asked if any of them would take service at a lower rate, and he said, "Yes, the Páshá has the power of fixing their wages as low as sixteen rupees." I said, "If I engaged some Turks as servants, could I take them to Bhopál?" He replied, "When I have asked the Páshá I shall be able to give you an answer." After this, I remarked, "In the performance of our religious observances, five sacred duties are enjoined: viz.—that we should have clean clothes, a clean body, a clean spot to worship in, clean water for ablution, and that we should be punctual to time. Now, in Mecca, the people wear very dirty clothes; what is the reason of this?" Súlimán Beg replied, "Caravans of people come from all parts of the world, and, of course, there are many poor among them; and as they cannot afford to buy new clothes, they are obliged to wear old and dirty ones. How could the Páshá clothe them all?" I replied, "There is no necessity for the Páshá to supply them with clothes; he has only to make better arrangements for their comfort—for instance, he should entertain a great many washermen,[1] and reduce the rate of prices for washing.[2] He should give strict orders to his servants not to wear dirty clothes, and should guide his subjects in the right way, decreeing that cleanliness is expected. When the people have been taught comfort and cleanliness after this fashion, they will begin to practise it of their own accord, and will bring up their children in the same habits." He replied, "I will tell the Páshá what you say," and seemed very pleased.

[1] In India, men, and not women, are employed to do washing.

[2] That is reduce the price of the water used in washing.

I then said that I was very anxious to see the ladies of his household, but that the ship in which were the presents I had brought for them and for himself from my country had not yet arrived. When they did, I should call upon his ladies and present my gifts. He replied, "There is no necessity to give them presents, they are equally anxious to meet your Highness." I said, "I have brought presents for them, and God willing, they shall be distributed to everyone."

After this, Mahomed Húsen, the interpreter, wrote to say, "Yesterday, being Friday, the 28th Sh'abán, 1280, A.H., the Shêríf of Mecca sent word by me to the Nawáb Dowager Begum that, 'if she wished to pay him a visit, she could fix any hour she liked on that day for honouring him with her presence, and that whatever conveyance she required should be sent for her.' I sent a message to this effect to Her Highness by Miánjí Riás-ud-dín.

The Dowager Begum replied that 'she required no conveyance, and that she would visit the Shêríf after mid-day; but that she would wish him to send four or five people to escort her, in case the Fakírs having recognized her should create a disturbance.'

The Shêríf, in accordance with Her Highness' request, deputed twenty men to attend her. Her Highness started on foot for the Shêríf's house, accompanied by Nawáb Faujdár Mahomed Khán, Mufti Sahib, and Miánjí Riás-ud-dín, four or five men servants and the same number of women servants. The Shêríf sent two of his Turkish attendants as the Istikbál, to receive her at some distance from the door, and on her arrival he himself conducted her with great courtesy and respect into the house, and had her shown into the Zenána. Nawáb Faujdár Mahomed Khán, myself and all the suite were first invited into the gentlemen's apartments on the lower floor, and afterwards were conducted to the upper-storied room, the Shêríf conversing with us very pleasantly and politely. He also made many inquiries for your Highness. After this we were served with sherbet and coffee, and the Shêríf went into the Zenána to see the Dowager Begum, returning after a little while to sit with us. In the meantime Her

Highness had sent to her servants for a large bag of rupees and a small one of gold mohurs;[1] but I neither know how many there were, nor to whom they were given. After this Her Highness left and went to the house of the Shêríf's sister, accompanied by us all; the Shêríf sending three more slaves with the suite, and giving orders that Nawáb Faujdár and all of us should be conducted to his brother-in-law's. The Dowager Begum went into the Zenána, and the Nawáb and party sat with the brother-in-law. After this, Her Highness returned to her own house, and gave me twenty rupees as a present for the three slaves, to whom I handed them, informing the Shêríf of the same."

[1] A gold mohur is worth about sixteen rupees, or thirty-two shillings.

CHAPTER XIII.

THE inhabitants of Mecca now began to say that I ought to pay visits to the Shêríf and Páshá, they being the rulers of the country; and I accordingly made up my mind to send my prime minister to wait upon the Shêríf. I wrote to the Naib Bakshí, and desired him to inform the Shêríf and Páshá that after the ship with my retinue had arrived, I would, God willing, pay them a visit, but that meantime, with their permission, I would depute the agreeable duty to Jumál-ud-dín Khán, my prime minister, who was the chief official in my dominion of Bhopál, and a most faithful servant of the state. The Naib Bakshí wrote in reply, that the Shêríf would receive him at half-past eleven o'clock that day, and the Páshá in the afternoon.

The minister went at eleven o'clock, accompanied

by the Naib Bakshí, to pay the Shêríf a visit, and on his return, gave me the follow-account of it:—"The Shêríf left the room where he was sitting, and received me in another, and, speaking in Arabic, asked after your Highness' health. I replied, 'Thanks be to God, Her Highness is well, and she desires me to thank you on her behalf, and to say that her ship, with all her people, is on its way, and, God willing, will probably cast anchor in Jeddah to-day. As soon as Her Highness' suite shall have arrived here, and her mind be relieved of all anxiety, she will visit you.' He replied, 'The Begum is a Guest sent by God, and the duties of hospitality devolve upon me. It is right, therefore, that I should show her all the honour and respect in my power. It is God's good pleasure, and the command of my ancestor His Prophet, upon whom be peace! The Begum is under no obligation to me.'

I then made my offering of the five or six guineas that your Highness had given me for the purpose, and the Shêríf, in taking them, said, 'I accept these out of respect for the entiquette of your country, although it is not the custom here.'

After this he called for coffee, of which I partook, and then took my leave, the Shêríf desiring me to give your Highness his salám.[1]

At my visit to the Páshá to-day, in accordance with your Highness' orders, I was accompanied by the Naíb Bakshí and Mahomed Húsen, your Highness' vakeel (or agent). On my arrival the Páshá inquired for your Highness' health, and I replied, 'The Begum sends her salám, and desires me to thank you cordially for your courtesy in having sent your son to Hada to receive and visit her.' He replied, 'It is my duty to show you all the politeness in my power.' I then partook of the lemon sherbet and coffee which were served, and proceeded to make my offering of the five guineas your Highness had given me for the purpose. The Páshá, seeing the guineas in my hand, said, in a surprised tone, 'Such a proceeding as this is very improper; you must not do this!' I replied, 'It is the custom of my country, and among us whoever pays a visit to a person of rank, makes an offering as a tribute of respect.' He said, 'I

[1] To send a salám is the same as sending one's compliments.

consider it disgraceful.' And as I saw from his countenance that he would be vexed, I did not give the guineas. The whole of this conversation was carried on through the medium of Mahomed Húsen the interpreter, we speaking Turkish and Hindustani respectively. I then took my leave, the Páshá rising with all due politeness, and sending his salám to your Highness."

After this, I made enquiries of the Arab Háji Mahomed Húsen regarding the etiquette observed in the visits of people of rank, and he gave me the following particulars:—"When the son, or son-in-law of the Páshá of Mecca goes to pay a visit to any Indian nobleman, the latter having risen from his seat, receives the guest with politeness. The compliment of serving sherbet and coffee is then observed; and a vessel filled with rose-water being brought in, the guests are sprinkled with it. Then, incense composed of ambergris and other sweet-scented things, is lighted in a burner and carried in front of the guests, and they hold their hands over the perfumed smoke. In the houses of Hindustani noblemen, these ceremonies are performed by people appointed by them for the purpose. At the conclusion of the visit, the host rises, and having made a salám, gives his guests permission to depart."

I now wrote to the Naib Bakshí, and told him that whatever day the Shêríf should appoint for my visit, I would hold myself in readiness for it. The Naib Bakshí wrote in reply, "The Shêríf says, 'If the Nawáb Sikandar Begum will honour me with her company, I shall be delighted to see her the day after tomorrow, on the 14th of the month, at eleven o'clock in the evening.'" I observed in reply, that "it was not our custom to pay visits at night, especially in the sacred month of Ramzán, which is the time for religious exercises; and I begged, therefore, to propose Wednesday, after mid-day prayer, as a more convenient time for my visit." The Shêríf, in answer to this wrote, through the Naib Bakshí, to say that, "if I went in the day-time the custom of giving me coffee and sherbet, which was an invariable one among Shêrífs and people of rank, could not be observed on account of the season of Ramzán; his wish was, therefore, that I should go at about nine or ten in the evening; but I was to do as I pleased, and he would be satisfied." I replied, "After nine o'clock in the evening, when I shall have read the prayers appointed for that hour, I will go to the Shêríf's." Accordingly, on the 16th of Ramzán, after nine o'clock in the evening, I went, as arranged, to pay my visit, and will now proceed to describe it.

CHAPTER XIV.

I WENT on foot to the Shêríf's house, and learnt that he was sitting alone in one of his rooms. Three slaves met me, and requested me to go into the Zenána, which I proceeded to do, they leading the way. At the first step of the staircase to the Zenána, some slaves were stationed; three or four steps higher up, some female Georgian attendants, and at the same distance still higher up, were some female Egyptians, servants of the mother and sisters of the Shêríf. These women placed their hands under my arms, and assisted me up the steps. Four or five steps higher up was one of the Shêríf's wives, and at the same distance, again, another wife. Then, beyond a door leading into a passage, at the place established by custom, being about half-way down the room, was the Shêríf's mother. As each of the Shêríf's wives met me, they first took my hand in theirs, and then putting their faces against both sides of my face and neck, they ended with kissing me lightly on my lips. The Shêríf's mother did the same.

Nawáb Faujdár Mahomed Khán, the Minister, Háfiz Mahomed Khán and Captain Mittú Khán who all accompanied me, were received in the gentlemen's apartments, and were joined by the Shêríf.

An hour afterwards some slaves came to me to say, that the Shêríf would, with my permission, come into the Zenána. I replied: "It is the Shêríf's own house," (meaning to say, "of course, he can do as he pleases.") I was sitting with his mother and wives, and conversing with the former, who spoke Arabic, J'afir Effendi's wife interpreting for us. The Shêríf has seven wives, four of whom I saw. Of these, two were Georgians, very handsome and beautifully dressed, being, one might say, literally covered with diamonds from head to foot. Their heads were encircled with a wreath, composed of jewels, and when the ladies moved or talked, the sparkling effect of these was very pretty. Underneath this diadem, they wore on their heads very small, fine handkerchiefs, such as English ladies carry in their hands; these were thickly embroidered with jewels, and tied in a coquettish way. From their neck to their waist, they were adorned with gems in the same fashion. Altogether, in face, height, and beauty of limbs, these two Georgians were as perfect women as one could wish to see. The dress of one was composed of black satin, and that of the other of lilac satin, embroidered with stars. The third wife was an Arabian, and had regular features. The fourth was an Abyssinian.

Those wives only who have borne children to the Shêríf are allowed to sit down in his presence, while those who have no family, are compelled to stand with their hands put together.[1]

When the Shêríf came into the Zenána, the four wives and the mother rose respectfully, and I, having marked their obeisance, advanced a few steps to meet him. After the Shêríf was seated I made my offering, and then followed the usual complimentary speeches. Having enquired for my health, the Shêríf

[1] This is an oriental attitude of respect observed by servants and inferiors towards people of rank.

asked: "How far is Bhopál from here?" I replied: "It is the Paradise of India—your Highness should pay it a visit." The Shêríf laughed and said: "My home is the K'abah."[1] After this, the wives and mother having again made their obeisance, sat down in the background.

Some Georgians and Africans who were in attendance, now brought in cups of coffee and pomegranate sherbet, and others the rose water and incense. Just as it is the fashion in India to give 'atar[2] and rose water, so is it the custom in Mecca to fumigate the guests with sweet-scented incense.

The Shêríf now said to me: "If your Highness will allow me, I will send for your uncle, the minister, and other gentlemen to come here." I replied: "I came here for the express purpose of paying a visit to the ladies of your Highness' family, and if the gentlemen come, they will go away. I had rather be with the ladies." The Shêríf, however, persevered in his wish to send for them, so, after a

[1] *i.e.* The Sanctuary at Mecca.

[2] 'Atar is a very strong perfume—such as oil of roses or sandalwood.

little while, I consented. The ladies accordingly withdrew, and some slaves were sent to fetch the gentlemen of my suite. The Shêríf did not salute any of them, but they, having made their salám, and kissed his hand, sat down. After a few complimentary speeches, they all returned to the gentlemen's apartments. The Shêríf remained sitting where he was. I should think his age was rather more than fifty.

The ladies now came into the room again, and, after remaining a little while longer, the Shêríf took leave of me and returned to the gentlemen's apartments. I then took leave of the ladies, and went to another house to visit the Shêríf's sisters. The party consisted of three sisters, four mothers,[1] two sisters-in-law, and a number of other women. After the usual complimentary speeches, the Shêríf's younger brother came and sat with us, and then coffee and sherbet were served. After the incense burning I took my departure, and returned to my own house. It is

[1] These were probably the mother of the Shêríf (who might have left his house to be present) and the mothers of his sisters—but the Begum does not particularize.

the custom at these visits for the men to embrace each other, and for the women to do the same among themselves.

When I arrived at my house, I enquired of Mahomed Húsen, the interpreter, what the etiquette was regarding the kissing of the Shêríf's hand, which ceremony he had observed at his visit. The interpreter replied,—"It is the custom here, when a person of rank visits the Shêríf, that the former should kiss the latter's hand. People of less importance only kiss the Shêríf's garments, while those of a still lower grade—such as servants—kiss the chair of state. Such Bedouins as hold any appointment under the Shêríf, being of the same tribe as himself, kiss his hand. Foot soldiers kiss the back of his shoulders."

After this, I wrote to the Páshá through Captain Mittú Khán, to say that whatever day he should appoint for my visit, I would go to him. The Páshá replied that, "on that very day, after prayers, I could honour him with my presence; and I was to be pleased to believe that he was very desirous of meeting me."

Accordingly, on the 20th Ramzán, at the appointed hour—being after nine o'clock in the evening—I went to pay my visit to the Páshá, and the arrangements regarding it were intrusted to his Turkish servants. They conducted my suite into a separate apartment, and then led me to one which had been prepared for my reception. The Páshá received me, and requested me to sit down on a chair, but seeing there were only a few chairs, I declined doing so, and sat down on a kind of ottoman, covered with a carpet. The ladies who accompanied me also sat down. After this the Páshá said, that with my permission, he would send for the gentlemen of my suite, and I assented. J'afir Effendi acted as interpreter, and the conversation consisted of the usual polite speeches.

Súlimán Beg, the Páshá's son, had come to the door of the house to receive me.

I should say the Páshá's age was a little more than sixty.

After the accustomed interchange of compliments, I asked permission to go into the Zenána, and the Páshá's son conducted me thither.

I was received by the ladies in the same manner as at my visit to the Shêríf's family.

Most of the women were Turkish, and all handsome, but the one pre-eminently so was the wife of Súlimán Beg. The ladies' dresses were not so richly ornamented with jewels as were those of the Shêríf's wives. The Páshá has two wives: one a Georgian, the other a Turkish woman. His son has one wife, also Turkish. They observed the same ceremonious politeness towards their husbands as did the Shêríf's wives towards him.

CHAPTER XV.

I NOW wrote to the Naib Bakshí, and said that I would send him and the minister, any day that the Shêríf might appoint, to present the offerings I had brought for them from Bhopál. These gentlemen replied, "That the next day, at two o'clock, after mid-day prayers, they would be glad to receive them;" and the Shêríf added, "It is necessary that I should be furnished this evening with a list, in Arabic, of the presents, and a detailed account of their value. I can then give permission for such things as are appropriate offerings to be sent; a repetition will thus be avoided of what occurred in the case of the Dowager Begum's presents, which had to be returned. That lady offered an affront to me, by sending more costly presents to Shebí Sáhib than to myself. I will willingly accept the Begum's presents, provided they are not inferior to those received by any one else."

I then desired the minister, in company with Háfiz Mahomed Khán, the Naib Bakshí, and Captain Mittú Khán, to wait upon the Shêríf and Páshá, and present my offerings, reporting to me, afterwards, any conversation that might take place.

I wrote, also, to Shêríf Abdúlla, and said that I was sending him a tray[1] of curiosities, and a similar one for his brother; also some bales of cloth for the other members of his family. "If he accepted them," I said, "I should be greatly obliged, and I hoped he would be pleased to do so."

I wrote to the same effect to the Páshá and his son respecting the presents for them.

The minister having distributed my gifts, reported, on his return, as follows:—"To-day, after mid-day prayer, accompanied by the other officers, as directed by your Highness, I waited on the Páshá with the presents. Having looked at the saddle-cloths, embroidered with gold, he said, 'I have never seen

[1] It is the custom in India to present gifts on trays.

such embroidery before—they do not make saddle-cloths like this in Constantinople.'

"After he had seen all the things, and the bag containing 1000 riáls, he said, 'I am not allowed to accept such gifts as these; if people of my own race make similar presents, I keep them, but the order is, if a Chief from another country comes here and makes me such offerings, I should keep them by me in order to avoid giving him offence and report the matter to Government, pending further orders. I will, therefore, keep all these presents, and send the list of them, with the Begum's letter, to Constantinople. In about two months I shall have received an answer, and I will inform the Begum of its purport.' I then said that the horse for which the trappings had been sent, would arrive immediately. On seeing the needlework prayer-carpet, made by your Highness' own hands, he was very pleased and astonished, and praised it greatly. When Captain Mittú Khán took the horse up to him, he began to ask him about Indian horses, and inquired which breed was the best in India. Mittú Khán replied, 'At the present time, all the principal chiefs ride Arab horses, and are great admirers of them.' He replied, 'There is no breed of horses like them.' Mittú Khán then observed that 'there were no mares exported from Arabia.' The Páshá then asked about the age of horses, and inquired 'in what district the longest-lived ones were to be found, and how long they were fit for work.' Mittú Khán replied, that 'the Arabs were longer-lived and stronger than Indian horses.' He again asked, 'which was the best breed in India?' and Mittú Khán replied, 'that raised in the Deccan—the Deccan horses are the handsomest and swiftest.' The Páshá then enquired about carriage horses and Mittú Khán said, 'Although other kinds are used for driving, the Arabs are the best; the chiefs prefer them to any other.' "

CHAPTER XVI.

After this, Súlimán Beg, the Páshá's son, came to pay me a second visit, on the occasion of the 'Íd-ul-Fitar.[1] I asked him if he was going to Constantinople? He replied: "In three or four days, but I will come and see you again before I start." I then asked who would carry on my work with the Páshá during his absence? He replied: "Now that you have visited him, and your mutual friendship is cemented, what necessity is there for agents to act in your respective interests?" He then told me the Páshá had sent his salám, and desired him to enquire after my health. I asked, "Whether or not there would be any impropriety in sending my 'salám' to the Sultan

[1] A festival held when the Ramzán ceases.

of Turkey?" He answered, "It is not the custom to do so, but there could be no harm in it." I rejoined: "When you go, then, say to the Sultan that a woman who has come to Mecca from India sends him her best 'salám.' " He said: "But I shall not have an interview with the Sultan—he only receives people of the very highest rank." I asked: "With what noble of distinction he (Súlimán Beg) would have an interview?" and in reply he mentioned some one's name that I cannot recollect, and said he would pay a visit to him. I then requested him to send my message through him, to which he replied: "Very well."

On the second day of the 'Íd-ul-Fitar, being the second of the month Shawwál, the Páshá of Mecca came to my house to pay me a visit. After enquiring for his health, I asked: "Who had given him the medal he wore on his uniform?" He answered: "It was given me by a former sovereign," and mentioning the name of a Sultan of Constantinople, he added: "It was not from Sultan Abdúl Azíz. If, however, I approve myself to him, I shall receive one from him, and people have recommended me to apply for it, but I have not done so yet. The present Sultan has a great liking for four things, and they are cannons, guns, ships, and road-making." I enquired if the Sultan had any railways or telegraphs in his country? "Yes, in Egypt, that is between Suez and Alexandria; and also in other places." "But why does he not establish them between Mecca and Medina, and Jeddah and Mecca?" "The Russians give us too much to do at present for that," he answered. I then remarked, that of all public works, the telegraph was the most important, and that, if there were one between Mecca and Constantinople, he would be able to have replies upon every subject without delay, and be guided in his actions accordingly. To this observation he made no answer. After this, as the gentlemen of my suite were dressed in uniform for the durbar, the Minister pointed out to the Páshá what uniform was worn in my army by both cavalry and infantry, and he made some of the officers stand in front of the Páshá, to show it to him. I then asked when his son Súlimán Beg started for Constantinople, and he replied, in three or four days. I said: "It is hot weather for him to travel in."

"It will be very cold the other side of Suez," he replied. After coffee and sherbet had been served, and the ceremony of fumigating had been gone through, he took his leave.

CHAPTER XVII.

I LEARNT afterwards through Niáz-Gul Khán, a Sowar of Bhopál, that the inhabitants of Mecca were commenting with much surprise on the Páshá's visit to me, and remarking, that hitherto no chief from Hindústán had received a visit from the Páshá as I had done, and they added: "Such an independent and accomplished chief as the Begum of Bhopál has never been in Mecca before."

When the Páshá came to pay his visit, I sent with the Istikbál, seven officers, nine Sowars, and fourteen foot soldiers. He told Mittú Khán that he had some guns of the new pattern, with conical bullets, coming to him, and they were on their way. He then enquired about the rifles we used, and how far they carried? Mittú Khán replied that "they would kill at a distance of 150 or 200 paces."

The Naib Bakshí, whom I had sent to enquire for the health of the Shêríf, and to congratulate him on the occasion of the 'Íd-ul-Fitar, reported that he had also thanked him on my behalf for his attention in sending his brother to meet me at the Istikbál. The Shêríf, in reply, sent his "salám" to me, and his congratulations on the occasion of the festival, and of my having accomplished the pilgrimage—he added: "The Begum has honoured us with her presence in Mecca, but I am ashamed to think of the small amount of courtesy and attention I have been able to show her. God willing, however, I will pay her a visit at whatever hour she may appoint."

I now deputed Captain Mittú Khán and the Naib Bakshí to invite the Shêríf and Páṣhá to an entertainment I was desirous of giving them on the occasion of the 'Íd, and in commemoration of my pilgrimage. The Páshá in reply said: "The only feast I require is a continuance of our present friendly relations." He then dismissed Mittú Khán, but detained the interpreter, to enquire of him what sort of entertainment would be given. In consequence of this, I wrote to the Shêríf and said: "I was anxious to give an entertainment in celebration of the 'Íd, and in commemoration of my pilgrimage, but as my people neither understood cooking after the fashion he was accustomed to, nor knew what dishes he admired, I would propose sending him the sum to be expended in a dinner, that he might have the food prepared as he liked." The Páshá wrote in reply: "That the Government would give him permission to acquiesce in my proposal."

I accordingly wrote to the Shêríf and Páshá, and said that I was sending them each 1000 riáls[1] for the entertainment which I hoped they would accept. Of this sum, I told the Páshá I wished 500 riáls expended on a dinner for himself, his son Súlimán Asaf Beg, and the remainder of his family and dependents, in celebration of the festival, and in commemoration of my pilgrimage; the remaining 500 I desired might be distributed among the officers and troops that had furnished guards and escorts for me.

[1] 1000 Riáls = to £225.

Both the Shêríf and Páshá accepted the money thus sent for the entertainment.

After this, I wrote to the Shêríf and Páshá about the position of my camp at 'Arfát, offering to pitch it wherever they might direct. I was informed by them that there were fixed places for the caravans from Syria and Egypt to encamp in, but that pilgrims from other countries might pitch their camps wherever they pleased. However, the Páshá proposed sending one of his people on the 1st of the month Zihíj with my camp to 'Arfát, to make arrangements for pitching it in a suitable place, in order that the utmost possible amount of comfort might be insured to me.

When I was starting for 'Arfát, I wrote to the Shêríf and Páshá, and asked them to make arrangements for furnishing a guard during my absence over the Shêríf's house in Mecca occupied by me, and to order a similar guard over the tents at 'Arfát, Muzdalifah and Mina.

They agreed to make arrangements for furnishing three guards—viz.: one at the house, another for the camp at 'Arfát, and a third for that at Mina; but they refused one for Muzdalifah. They further recommended me to put all the valuables I had into a box, and send them to the Imperial Treasury at Mecca, where they might remain in safety till my return. I replied that I had no valuables to make over to them.

I then proceeded to 'Arfát, and having completed the whole of the prescribed duties of the pilgrimage, I returned to the exalted Mecca.

The Shêríf, at the farewell visit he paid me, wore in his waist-belt two daggers, the handles of which were thickly set with diamonds. Six bosses of diamonds were very large, and I should say the price of the six could not have been less than six lakhs of rupees (£60,000).

The Pásha did not come to pay me a visit.

When I left Mecca the Shêríf and Páshá sent an escort of cavalry and infantry, with a relation of the Shêríf, as far as Haddah, with me. On my arrival at Jeddah, the English Consul, Mr Stanley, showed me great politeness and kindness, and sent, with the Istikbál, his own interpreter, and one of his trusty officials to receive me; he also himself paid me a visit, and said, on leaving, that two distinguished gentlemen of the French consulate were coming to pay me a visit, and he hoped I would receive them. I asked him why he had not brought them with him to introduce them, and he replied that "it was not etiquette to do so."

About two hours after this, the French and Abyssinian Consuls arrived. They were very intelligent, vivacious, good-looking young men, their faces beaming with eloquence, and they conversed in Arabic with great fluency. They asked me to tell them about my journey to Mecca, and I related all my adventures, and begged them to give my cordial greeting to the Emperor Napoleon, and to say that the pleasure of meeting the French Consul had been one of the advantages I had enjoyed from my visit to Mecca. After receiving the compliment of "'atar," the two gentlemen took their departure.

Having left Jeddah in the ship from Calcutta, which had been engaged for me by the Consul, I arrived at Aden, where we remained one day to take in coal, and then proceeded to Bombay.

Notwithstanding that the Páshá and Shêríf made

an outward show of politeness towards me, in their hearts they were displeased with me. I can imagine two reasons for their dislike, one of which was that they had both heard a great deal of my loyalty to the British Government during the time of the mutiny, from the late Nawáb (lit. "who is now in Paradise"), Faujdár Mahomed Khán, as well as from those people who had been driven away from India during those troublous times. The other reason was, that I one day remarked (being astonished at the habits of the people of Mecca, and the dirty condition of their houses), "The Sultan of Turkey gives thirty lakhs of rupees (£300,000) a-year for the expenses incurred in keeping up the holy places at Mecca and Medina. But there is neither cleanliness in the city, nor are there any good arrangements made within the precincts of the shrines. Now if the Sultan would give *me* those thirty lakhs, I would make arrangements for the Government of Bhopál to be carried on by my son-in-law and daughter, and you would see what a state of order and cleanliness *I* would keep the august cities in, and what arrangements *I* would make for the proper maintenance of the holy shrines; so that the Sultan would find out that dishonest people had been diverting his money from its legitimate uses, and had not kept a single thing in order; while I, in a few days, would effect a complete reformation!"

When I made this speech, J'afir Effendi, an employé in the Páshá's service, was present, as well as several other people of Mecca, so I think it likely some of them repeated it to the Shêríf and Páshá; more especially as, one day afterwards, during a visit of the latter, I perceived, from the tone of his conversation, that he was annoyed, for he remarked, "Some people come to the pilgrimage in a spirit of humility, and not with their heads lifted up; many others, who are obstinate and designing, also come, and what do they gain by it?"

Altogether, I felt convinced that he was angry with me for my speech. If he had been a man of liberal views, he would have been rather pleased than otherwise, and have asked me to explain what arrangements I thought were required.

CHAPTER XVIII.

I WILL now recapitulate my impressions of Mecca and Jeddah. The latter is a desolate-looking city, very dirty, and pervaded with unsavoury odours. The climate is damp, the atmosphere being steamy, but there are neither water-courses nor tanks of any size; some of them are mere ponds, having no depth; and the colour of the water is dirty, while there are a great many insects in it, but the taste of it is not very bad.

The city of Mecca is wild and melancholy-looking, and like all hilly places has a dreary, repulsive aspect. Sometimes the weather is cold, sometimes extremely hot. There is consequently a prevalence of dangerous and inflammatory diseases, and of catarrh. The nights, however, are very pleasant, being cool and healthy, without being cold, but an hour before sunrise, it begins to be as hot as in the daytime. The moonlight is magnificent, the atmosphere being free from moisture and clouds, and the horizon remaining perfectly clear. There is a scarcity of dew, and frequently a strong wind blows, and there is a good deal of thunder and lightning but very little rain; if any falls at all, it does not continue with any violence beyond an hour or two. Sometimes light clouds float about, occasionally causing shade, but at other times not moderating the sun's rays; and they never last more than two or three days. In some places green vegetables are grown, also melons and the Castor oil plant;[1] but the varieties of cucumbers and gourds which we have in India do not grow there. Fruit and vegetables, however, are to be had at all seasons of the year in Mecca, being brought thither from Ta'íf in great abundance. They are both better and sweeter than the fruit we get in India. There is not a single tree in the whole city of Mecca, the soil of which is very sandy, and there is a great

[1] Ricinus Communis, or Palma Christi.

scarcity of mould; what there is, is a mixture of light and dark.

In some of the wells in Mecca, water has only been found by digging deep; in others, nearer the surface. Some of it is brackish, but some good.

The air is not good, although in my opinion it might be, but for the stupidity and carelessness of the inhabitants, who allow accumulations of dirt to taint and vitiate it. This nuisance is caused by the myriads of camels, goats and sheep which are brought into Mecca, to be slaughtered and offered in sacrifice by the different caravans of pilgrims; and there are no arrangements made for preserving cleanliness by the removal of the offal.

The men and women have dreadfully harsh voices; their heads and shoulders are, generally speaking, handsome, but the rest of their body is not well formed; they vary in height, some being tall and thin, others short and fat; while the women have even greater muscular strength than the men, and are large-made and noisy. The people take a great quantity of food, as much as 5 or 6 lbs. in weight in the course of the day, but their diet is very gross; and their habits are dirty. The strength of the men is such, that they are able to lift a weight of twelve maunds (960 lbs.), whereas no one in India ever carries more than three maunds; and this burden they will carry without any assistance to the top of a high house.

The colours of their complexion are various, some few people being fair, while others are sallow, orange-coloured, black, and of different hues. Their hair is generally light or golden, and seldom black, and most of the men have small beards, rather than bushy ones.

In character, the majority of the people are miserly, violent-tempered, hard-hearted, and covetous, and they are both awkward and stupid.

These are my impressions, after a sojourn of four months in the country. Had I remained there a year, I should doubtless have had a great deal more to record.

CHAPTER XIX.

I WISHED to continue my Pilgrimage to Medina, but before coming to any decision I wrote to Míán Faujdár Mahomed Khán, saying that I had heard most appalling accounts of the state of the road to Medina, "which, if true, will deter me from going to that place, the Pilgrimage to Medina not being obligatory on Mahomedans. I am further induced not to go for the following reasons:—

1st. That all the camels being shagdaf, it is impossible for any one to move a muscle when on them.

2nd. The roads are very bad.

3rd. I know no particulars regarding the route, or the country through which it passes.

4th. I know nothing of Arabic, or of the language and customs of the Bedouins, so cannot understand what they say, or what they do.

5th. I have very few troops with me.

6th. I have not sufficient money to engage an escort of the Shêríf's or Páshá's troops.

7th. Even if I had, the officers have no fixed pay, and would take all they could from me, and are, I believe, capable of plundering my property.

8th. The reputation of the Kudsíah Begum for wealth and liberality, is now so widely known, that she could not go *incog.* If we could by any means get away quietly, the Bedouins would be very angry, and would say: 'This is the very Begum who could spend so much money at Mecca, and yet is now travelling empty handed, for fear we should plunder her on the way!'

9th. The Bedouins demand Bukhsheesh at every step, and if they do not obtain money or food, frequently grossly insult, or even kill one. Where am I to find money to satisfy all their demands?

10th. The local authorities do not exert themselves to protect Pilgrims. The Shêríf takes two Ríáls from the Bedouins for every camel engaged; when he has collected a large number of Pilgrims, he sends them off to Medina, caring only for the money he is to receive, and nothing about the safety of the Pilgrims.

11th. The Shêríf, himself, never goes with a caravan, his servants told me it is not etiquette for him to do so, he sends a nephew or distant relative.

12th. I have a great number of women, and but few men in my suite, I should consequently require a large escort.

13th. I have heard that the Bedouins frequently have disputes with the Turkish Government, in which case, caravans are obliged to remain at Medina two or three months."

I also wrote to Hakím Bahár 'Alí Khán, as follows:—

"The Nawáb Kudsíah Begum, soon after her arrival at Mecca, unpacked her boxes, and dealt out her alms with indiscriminate liberality. Mián Faujdár Mahomed Khán and I, both told her that the beggars were chiefly people of bad character, and also that misfortune generally befell those who here earn a reputation for wealth. (In Mecca, no one gives charity openly, it is always done quietly and by degrees, as if the donors were poor.)

Her Highness, however, would listen to nothing we had to say, and continued to distribute her gifts as she thought fit, till even the Shêríf became displeased at her mode of giving alms, just in the same way as the people of Bhopál are.

We also told her that as it entirely depended on the good will of the Shêríf whether anyone could go to Medina or not, she should keep him in a good humour, the twelve Bedouin chiefs at the twelve stages being mostly relatives of his.

We also said to her: 'When the Bedouins hear of your liberality, they will demand, Heaven only knows how much from you!' We reminded her, too, of the Bedouins trying to carry her off on the way to Mecca, but she paid no heed to our remarks. Having heard of the dangers of the road, I wrote to Mián Faujdár Mahomed Khán, a copy of which letter I forward for your perusal.

A person from Joudhpore, by name Mústáh, has sent me an account of a friend of his, who visited Mecca, and whilst there had gained a reputation for generosity and wealth. The Bedouins seized him when on his way to Mecca, and made him pay a lakh of Rupees* before they released him. He added, 'as the Nawáb Kudsíah Begum is even better known than my friend, it would not be safe for her to go.'

A woman, by name Marían Bíbí, a widow of Runjeet-Sing, has also strongly advised me not to go.

As all my people are anxious to perform the Pilgrimage, and we have no reliable information to depend upon, I shall feel much obliged by your informing me of the real state of the road, &c., &c."

Mián Faujdár Mahomed Khán's reply was as follows:—

"What you write is quite true and most sensible; to go to Medina till the road is quite safe is to trifle with our lives. You are quite right not to go, for it is written in the Venerable Korán, 'it is wicked to put one's life in danger.'

"It is laid down that all Mahomedans ought to go to Mecca, but it is not necessary to go to

* Equal to £10,000.

Medina. When our Pilgrimage here is over, we should return to Bhopál."

Hakím Bakár 'Alí Khán also wrote:—

"My opinion quite coincides with your Highness's, you should not go to Medina. You may come here again some day, when you may be able to go. The Molvís, and men learned in the law, have decided that it is not necessary to go to Medina, if the roads are unsafe. Imám Mahomed Ghazálí has even forbidden it."

After this, my First Minister reported to me as follows:—"I went with Capt. Mittú Khán to the Páshá 'Izzat Ahmed, and he informed me that the Sultan had cleared the road to Medina, and that several caravans would shortly be going there. He added, 'I am averse to the Begum going along this road, because the fame of her wealth has been spread abroad, and the Bedouins will consequently give a great deal of trouble. If she goes, I will send her by the Eastern road with an escort and some guns, she would then be quite safe, and she should engage her camels to go by that route, and reduce her suite so as not to have more than 50 camels.'

"I replied to the Páshá, though the Interpreter, 'If there is fear of Bedouins on the Imperial road, there must be equal danger on the Eastern road; the Bedouins hearing of the Begum going by that route will be certain to lie in wait for her.' He said, 'There is far greater safety on the Eastern than on the Imperial road.' As he would not give any further answer to my question, I informed him I would report the matter to your Highness, and communicate to him your wishes. He then said, 'You should hire the camels and camel drivers through the Shêríf, as he is the Ruler and Spiritual Head of the Bedouins, he therefore knows the good and bad among them. I know nothing about the Bedouins.' I then took my departure and came to your Highness."

I again sent the Minister to the Shêríf and Páshá; and he said to the Shêrif: "The Begum of Bhopál is much distressed to hear that the Bedouins have closed the road to Medina." The Shêríf replied: "God willing, the road will soon be opened, I and the Páshá are not unmindful of the Begum's safety." The Páshá said: "Please God, the Begum will soon be able to visit Medina. I have written several letters to the Páshá of Medina, whose duty it is to keep the Bedouins in order, and I have also sent him troops. I expect in a few days to hear from him; directly I do so, I will inform the Begum. If the road is not safe, I will send a strong escort with artillery to accompany her."

When Sulimán Beg, the Páshá's son, paid me his second visit, he said: "Yesterday, the Shêríf and Páshá were in consultation, and they have arranged to send you by the Eastern road to Medina; you should reduce your caravan (of 700 camels) to about 50 or 100 camels, and you should leave all your valuables in Mecca." I replied: "Give my compliments to the Páshá, and ask him to *write* what you have now told me, and *I* will write and inquire of him regarding those points on which I want information." Sulimán Beg then became quite silent.

I then wrote to Shêríf Abdúllah and Páshá 'Izzat Ahmed, as follows:—

"I have made many inquiries regarding the road to Medina; some people tell me there are four roads, others, that there are five or six; some say the roads are open, others that they are all closed. I believe, therefore, that none of them know anything about the matter. I shall feel much obliged by your sending me a list of the various routes, together with the names of the marches on each, and also by your informing me what roads are closed and what open."

In reply, Shêríf Abdúllah and the Páshá wrote:—

"There are five roads to Medina, besides the Imperial road, (Mamba-ul-kher) but only small caravans of 40 or 50 camels go along most of them. The large caravans go either by the Imperial or Eastern road.

It is to be hoped that, through the efforts of the Páshá of Medina, the Imperial road will soon be clear of Bedouins."

I learned from Mahomed Hasan, an Arab, the following particulars regarding the routes, &c., to Medina:—

"About the 15th or 20th Shawwál, the first caravan leaves Mecca, it assembles at Wádí Fatima: owing to the scarcity of water, it goes in small parties to Safrá Wádí, (the seventh March from

Mecca). Many stop one day and night at Rai-ek, *en route.*

At Safrá Wádí, the caravan re-assembles, and marches together for two marches, as far as Bír Sharokí, for fear of the Bedouins. From Bír Sharokí, they go in small parties to Medina, which is one march distant.

In marching from Medina to Mecca, the same precautions are adopted.

After the "Hajj," two caravans go from Mecca to Medina; the first is called Tíárah, and goes with the Syrian caravan; the second starts about twenty days after, and goes very slowly."

Amír Baksh, an inhabitant of Mecca, gave the following reply to my inquiries:—"The Imperial, Eastern, and Suez roads are all infested with Bedouins, those on the Eastern road obey the Shêríf of Mecca, consequently, they do not do any harm. The Suez route is not necessarily entirely by land; from Suez and Jeddah, the journey to Khárí Amboh can be performed in a steamer or sailing vessel."

I wrote, as follows, to Miriam Bíbí, of Aden,

whose orders all the Bedouins respect, (twelve of the Bedouin chiefs being under Sheikh S'ad, who is her disciple.)

"I have heard from the people at Mecca that the roads to Medina are closed, because there is a dispute between the Bedouins and the Sultan of Turkey. I have also been informed that Sheikh S'ad, who is a great chief among the Bedouins, is your disciple. I write, therefore, to request that you will give me a letter to Sheikh S'ad, to the effect that when my caravan goes from Mecca to Medina, he, or his son, or one of his near relatives, should accompany and escort it safely to Medina and back again to Mecca. I will handsomely reward him. Please send the letter for Sheikh S'ad to me, and I will forward it to him and receive his reply."

I wrote to H. B. M's Consul at Jeddah, as follows:

"I send herewith copies of all the reports I have received regarding the routes to Medina. Please give me your advice. I propose going with the Egyptian and Syrian caravan to Medina, and, having performed the Pilgrimage, to go with the same caravan to Suez, from whence I hear I can proceed by steamer, *viâ* Aden, to Bombay. I cannot learn anything here about the route from Medina to Suez,—which I believe is about 27 marches. Will you kindly inform me whether supplies can readily be obtained, whether the road is safe, and also whether you can procure me an escort."

The Consul wrote in reply:—

"There are hundreds of persons in Mecca who know far more about the routes than I do; as, however, you have asked my advice, I should recommend you to march to Jeddah, and to go from there to Khárí Amboh by steamer; from Khárí Amboh it is not many marches to Medina.

"I have learned the following, regarding the Suez road, from the people here. The road is bad, water is scarce, the distance great, and the expense will be enormous. It is 600 British miles from Medina to Suez, and I should advise you *not* to go by that route: if, however, you are bent on going to Suez, your best plan would be this:—

"From Medina to Khárí Amboh by land, and thence to Suez by steamer. If you wish it, I will arrange to charter one of the Imperial (Turkish) steamers for you. From Suez to Bombay you will, I fear, encounter difficulty, as there are only two or three of the Peninsular and Oriental Company's steamers even there. In my opinion, it would be better for you to charter a steamer in Bombay to fetch you.

"The person who advised you to march from Mecca to Suez, and thence by steamer to Bombay, did so from interested motives.

"There is no doubt the Eastern road from Mecca to Medina is the safest, but even on it men and animals suffer great inconvenience.

"This being a foreign country, I am unable to order an escort for you."

I received a letter from Sheikh S'ad in reply to the one sent him by Miríam Bíbí; he wrote thus:—

"I send my son Hazífá to you, he will do all you desire, and convey you in all safety and comfort. I will do all I can to assist you. Pray treat my son, and the Arabs with him, with all kindness, because they will suffer much trouble and inconvenience. Your generosity is well known.

"The camel men will receive every assistance from me, and my son will study your comfort in every way."

On further inquiry, I learned that the marches are thus performed:—

The caravan marches daily for seven "Pahars,"* and halts for one "Pahar." In this manner Medina is reached in twelve days.

There is no water on the road. The Bedouins alone know the route, and where any water is to be found.

There are many hills on the road to Medina, but all destitute of trees.

Whatever the Pilgrims take with them the Bedouins seize, giving back only what they do not want.

Even the water which is carried on camels they sometimes seize. They will convey in safety to Medina any caravan with which they are pleased, but if they are annoyed, they leave the caravan and disappear among the Hills; and the Pilgrims, not knowing the

* A "Pahar" or Watch is equal to three hours.

road, wander about till they die from thirst and starvation.

The Bedouins, for five out of the twelve stages to Medina, acknowledge the Shêríf Abdúlla, for the other seven they look to Sheikh S'ad as their Ruler.

But they only obey the orders of their chiefs so long as it suits them, no reliance is to be placed in them, they respect no promises, and obey no orders, unless it pleases them to do so.

For these reasons, I resolved not to go to Medina, as it would have been needlessly risking my own life and those of my suite.

I learned that the coverings for the shrines at Mecca and Medina are sent with a large body of troops, which accompanies the Syrian and Egyptian caravans; that caravan is therefore never molested.

APPENDIX 1

LOCALITY. At the end of the suburbs of Mecca. Holy place. The mosque of the holy 'Ayeshah.

This Mosque is built at about six miles distance from the sacred shrine, at a place called Tan'ayím, and the mosque itself is a little beyond the boundary of the shrine (Had-i-Haram). Hence they enter on the pilgrimage, and the manner of doing so is as follows: Having proceeded to this mosque, they undertake the pilgrim vows and habit, and having made two voluntary prayers, with prostrations, they then proceed towards the shrine, repeating the word "Labaik"[1] on their way thither. After entering the city of Mecca, they next make the circuit of the shrine; then they visit the place of Abraham (within the shrine), and there, also, make two voluntary prayers, with prostrations. Thence they proceed to the hill of Safá and Marwah, and perform the running (S'aí); and after that the men perform the Halak (shaving the head), and the women the Kasar (clipping the hair). This is the ceremonial of the *'Umrah* (pilgrimage), and is obligatory on all Mussalmáns. In performing it it is usual to go on foot, but some ride.

The Sikandar Begum and her whole suite of attendants visited this mosque, and performed the

[1] "Labaik"—*I am present*—the old Hebrew expression, "Here am I."

pilgrimage ('Umrah). This, moreover, is a general rule, that as long as one continues to live in the city of Mecca, and within the sacred boundary he is freed from the obligation of undergoing the duties and vows of the pilgrimage ('Umrah); but should he leave the boundary (for any purpose), and afterwards return to Mecca, he cannot enter the city before again undergoing this course. And, moreover, whoever goes to Mecca before the month Shawwál, and continues to remain in the city, is considered a resident of Mecca, and from that month the residents of Mecca are freed from the obligations of performing the pilgrimage ('Umrah). The only means of riding at Mecca, for all ordinary people and travellers, is on donkeys, and this, moreover, is a proper style of riding for all orthodox believers.[2] The Sikandar Begum, accordingly, purchased a couple of these animals, and her attendants used them for performing the 'Umrah. As was said before, this pilgrimage of 'Umrah commences from the mosque of Hodebiah, which is situated in a plain at the foot of the mountain Tan'ayún. The merciful Prophet gave directions to (his wife) the holy 'Ayeshah to perform the Umrah from that spot; and, accordingly, those of the orthodox (Sunnat-u-Jamáat) creed continue to do the same; but seceders (the Sheeah sect) do not acknowledge the duty of going to this mosque.

[2] Allusion is made here to the practice of Mahommad generally using this animal, and his example has conferred dignity upon it.

APPENDIX 2

LOCALITY. The same. [i.e. Within the sacred boundary]. Holy place. Matáf (or Place of Circuit.)

The mode of performing the Toáf is as follows:

The pilgrimages start from the Black Stone (Aswad) which is embedded in a gold setting in a corner of the house of God, and thence as they make the circuit, they continue to offer devotions and to repeat verses of the blessed Korán suitable to the occasion. Having made the circuit, and arrived again at the Black Stone, uttering the formula, "In the Name of God, who alone is Great (Bism-Illáh-Allahuh Akbar) they kiss the Black Stone. Close to it is the spot where the holy Ishmáel, may the Peace of God, &c., and of his mother, the Lady Hagar, lie buried. In the above manner, the circuit is repeated seven times, and together the whole ceremony is termed a Toáf; while every separate circuit is called a Shuát (one turn). Whilst making the first three turns, men stand up straight, throwing the chest well forward, but the next four they make in their usual way of walking. Each one, immediately in his entrance into Mecca, goes to perform the Toáf. This is called the "Toáf-ul-Kudúm," or the first Toáf, and also the Toáf-ul-Wird (of alighting), and Toáf-ul-Wárid (of arrival); and the performance of this Toáf is obligatory among the orthodox.

The next takes place after the Haj has been completed, and this second one has six names. They are as follows:-

1. Toáf-uz-Ziyárat (of the holy places)
2. Toáf-í-dín (of the faith.)
3. Toáf-i-Ifazah (of grace, or salvation.)
4. Toáf-ul-Haj (of the pilgrimage.)
5. Toáf-ul-Farz (of obligation.)
6. Toáf-i-Yaum-un-Nahár (of the day of sacrifice, because at the end of the Haj they usually sacrifice a camel.)

The second Toáf is regarded as a chief pillar of the Haj, *i.e.*, until this has been performed, although every other part of the Haj may have been accomplished, without this, it is as good as unfulfilled. Its performance is fixed for the day when the pilgrimages return from Arfát, after the completion of the rest of the Haj.

The occasion of the third Toáf is a taking leave of Mecca. This has three names, as follows, viz.:-

1st. Toáf-us-Sadr.

2nd. Toáf-ul-Wad'aa (departure.)

3rd. Toáf-ur-Rujú'a (returning.)

And this is performed on the eve of departure, after having finished every other rule and duty of the Haj,- and in the act of starting to return home. The mode of making this Toáf is as follows:- after completing the Toáf, they drink of the water of Zamzam, and kiss the doorway of the house of God, and then depart, withdrawing from the holy house backwards, till they reach the circle of the Toáf, looking after the time towards the shrine. This is the time specially fixed for this Toáf to take place, and it also is considered to be right and desirable to be performed.

The fourth Toáf is that of 'Umrah, called so after the mosque of that name, Toáf-ul-'Umrah. It is obligatory, on the occasion of making the pilgrimage of 'Umrah.

The fifth Toáf is that of Nazr; and the intent of this is, that any one who makes a vow to God for the attainment of some particular object, to the effect that he will perform some sacred act, on obtaining the object of his wishes, makes this Toáf.

The sixth is the Toáf-un-Tahaiyah. Those who have not been able to perform the circuit above-named make this.

The seventh is the Toáf-un-Nafalí. This is voluntary, and may be performed at any time, there being no fixed day; but if anyone undertake it, he is bound to complete it after having once commenced. After every time of prayers, each one as he is able makes this Toáf, once, twice, or oftener. Moreover, during the performance of this one, it is permitted to refresh oneself with spices, or something agreeable.

The hours for daily prayers at the shrine are five times for men and for old women, and it is obligatory on them to attend; but for women who are still behind the screen (pardahdár), three times are considered to be sufficient, viz.: before sunrise (Súbh), at sunset

(Maghrib), and from night till 4 A.M. ('Ishá), at which times they are bound to go to prayers at the shrine. These times are prescribed as sufficient for them, because of preserving the security of the veil, which is necessary for young women; otherwise there is no prohibition in the matter.

The old, feeble, and sick, who cannot get as far as the shrine, may pay their devotions at home, or at the nearest mosque; but this is not allowable for those that are young, and in full health; such are required to go to the Ka'ábah at the five hours prescribed, and perform their devotions there. On entering the doorway, they must stoop and kiss the threshold, and bend down their head upon it, repeating prayers and verses from the blessed Word of God, and offering up prayers for the spiritual and temporal prosperity of all Mussulmáns.

For the interval from 9 P.M. to 5 A.M. there are five divisions appointed, and when these five have passed the true dawn (Súbh Sádik) is said to begin; *i.e.* about an hour before sunrise.

Besides the black stone in the Ka'ábah, there is also another, called Rukn-i-Yemaní, which is fixed in a different corner of the shrine. This they only stretch out the hand to touch, and having done so, they then kiss their hand.

AFTERWORD

MUSLIM WOMEN WRITE THEIR JOURNEYS ABROAD

Siobhan Lambert-Hurley

FOR tales of Muslim women travellers out of South Asia, one need look no further than the archives of the Mughal and early colonial states. There, we find examples of Muslim women from a range of social backgrounds embarking on foreign journeys—from women of the Mughal court going on extended pilgrimage in the late sixteenth century to Muslim female servants and slaves accompanying their masters from the East India Company back to Britain.[1] Yet none of this evidence comes from the pens of women themselves. Only in the high colonial era—the period after the establishment of British crown rule in 1858—do Muslim women in South Asia appear to have begun writing about their journeys and publishing travel

[1] Abul Fazl, *Akbar-nama*, vol. III, tr. H. Beveridge (Calcutta: Asiatic Society, 1939), pp. 569-70; and Michael H. Fisher, *Counterflows to Colonialism: Indian Travellers and Settlers in Britain 1600-1857* (Delhi: Permanent Black, 2004), pp. 222-4.

accounts in ever-greater numbers.[2] This trajectory suggests, as noted in the Introduction, that the impetus to write about their experiences of travel was closely related to the establishment of colonial rule in the Indian subcontinent, even as a long tradition of travel writing existed within the Muslim world.[3] Travel writing by Muslim men in South Asia and Muslim women elsewhere in the Islamic world, as well as that by women of other communities within South Asia, has received at least limited attention in recent years;[4]

[2] I make this judgement on the basis of a comprehensive survey of Persian, Urdu and English archives in South Asia and Britain. At the same time, I recognise the possibility that earlier Muslim women's travel accounts may be found in South Asia, as they have been in Iran, in anthologies (*jung* and *majmu'a*) also containing letters, decrees, poems and essays. See Kathryn Babayan, '"In Spirit We Ate Each Other's Sorrow": Female Companionship in Seventeeth-Century Safavi Iran' in Kathryn Babayan and Afsaneh Najmabadi (eds.), *Islamicate Sexualities: Translations across Temporal Geographies of Desire* (Cambridge: Harvard University Press, forthcoming).

[3] For just a few examples of earlier travel writing within the Muslim world, see Michael Wolfe (ed.), *One Thousand Roads to Mecca: Ten Centuries of Travelers Writing About the Muslim Pilgrimage* (New York: Grove Press, 1997); Ross E. Dunn, *The Adventures of Ibn Battuta: A Muslim Traveller of the 14th Century*, rev. edn. (Berkeley: University of California Press, 2005); and part II of Dale F. Eickelman and James Piscatori (eds.), *Muslim Travellers: Pilgrimage, Migration, and the Religious Imagination* (London: Routledge, 1990).

[4] For a recent example of each of these types of studies, see Mushirul Hasan (ed.), *Westward Bound: Travels of Mirza Abu Taleb* (Delhi: Oxford University Press, 2005); Reina Lewis, *Women, Travel*

but to date no real attempt has been made to theorise on this type of literature produced by Muslim women in the South Asian context, suggesting that there is a kind of historiographical need for some kind of survey. In this short Afterword, then, I intend to provide a brief overview of foreign travel writing by Muslim women in South Asia in the modern period, as an introduction to the various sub-genres and the timeline of their production. The point of departure is Nawab Sikandar Begum's *A Pilgrimage to Mecca*, this book's primary focus, as it appears to be the first publication of this type.

A relevant feature of this early text within the context of this essay is that it may be seen to have inspired the author's granddaughter, Nawab Sultan Jahan Begum of Bhopal, to write a hajj account of her own upon her return from Mecca in 1904. Published in English translation under the title *The Story of a Pilgrimage to the Hijaz* in 1909,[5] it revealed some

and the Ottoman Harem (New Brunswick, New Jersey: Rutgers University Press, 2004); and Meera Kosambi, 'Introduction: Returning the American Gaze: Situating Pandita Ramabai's American Encounter' in *Pandita Ramabai's American Encounter: The Peoples of the United States (1889)* (Bloomington: Indiana University Press, 2003), pp. 3-46. Only Barbara Metcalf touches on Muslim women's travel writing in 'The Pilgrimage Remembered: South Asian Accounts of the Hajj' in Eickelman and Piscatori, *Muslim Travellers,* pp. 85-107.

[5] Sultan Jahan Begum, *The Story of a Pilgrimage to Hijaz* (Calcutta: Thacker, Spink & Co., 1909). An abbreviated account of this

curious differences between the two ruling Begums, particularly in terms of their understanding of religious orthodoxy and notions of 'centre' and 'periphery' within the Islamic world. While Sikandar expressed her view that many of the inhabitants of Arabia were, as she put it, 'totally ignorant'[6] of their faith, her granddaughter recounted a process by which she had been inspired by her journey to model her religious practice on a more Arabian-style Islam.[7] Their writings were rather more alike, however, in terms of qualities of introspection, neither really displaying the focus on 'individual experiences, perceptions, and feelings' that Metcalf has identified to be a feature of 'modern' hajj accounts.[8] Only in the later twentieth century did Muslim women from South Asia—three representative examples being Zainab Khatun Kakakhail from Pakistan, Saba Mustafa from India and Sabrina Q. Rashid from Bangladesh—begin publishing descriptions of hajj in

journey was also contained in her autobiography. See Sultan Jahan Begum, *An Account of My Life*, vol. II, tr. Abdus Samad Khan (Bombay: The Times Press, 1922), ch. XIV.

6 Sikandar, *Pilgrimage*, p. 73.

7 I have expanded on this point in 'Out of India: The Journeys of the Begam of Bhopal, 1901-1930', *Women's Studies' International Forum*, 21:3 (June 1998), pp. 263-76; reprinted in Tony Ballantyne and Antoinette Burton (eds.), *Bodies in Contact: Rethinking Colonial Encounters in World History* (Durham, NC: Duke University Press, 2005), pp. 293-309, especially pp. 299-300.

8 Metcalf, 'Pilgrimage Remembered', p. 87.

which their own 'inner experiences' were foregrounded.[9]

In terms of style, it may be noted that it was also in the twentieth century that shorter pieces on women's pilgrimages began appearing in journals and anthologies alongside full book-length accounts. A key example is those articles published in the Urdu women's magazine, *Tahzib un-Niswan*, by Tahzibi sisters (as readers and contributors were known) from the 1920s.[10] Another is Professor Sughra Mehdi's poetic and notably feeling-driven account in 'Mekhanon ka Pata' of 'drinking from the holy cup' when she visited Mecca, Medina and, as a Shia, Najaf, Karbala and other holy sites in Iraq and Iran in 1998.[11]

[9] Professor Zainab Khatun Kakakhail, *Jalwah gah-i-tauhid ke rubaru: Safar-i-hajj aur astana-yi nabuwwat par haziri ki rudad* (Lahore: Himayatul-Islam Press, 1976); Saba Mustafa, *Paharon ke daman men: Safanama-yi arz-i-muqaddas* (Banglaore: Alaktrik Qaumi Pres, 1979); Dr Sabrina Q. Rashid, *Hajj: A Wonderful Experience: With a Guide to Hajj* (Dhaka: Islamic Foundation Bangladesh, 2005). The former two works are discussed in Metcalf, 'Pilgrimage Remembered', pp. 91-2, 100.

[10] Gail Minault makes references to these short hajj accounts in *Secluded Scholars: Women's Education and Muslim Social Reform in Colonial India* (Delhi: Oxford University Press, 1998), p. 122. Unfortunately, my own incomplete survey of *Tahzib un-Niswan* collections in the Maulana Azad Library in Aligarh and the Sundarayya Vignana Kendram in Hyderabad has failed, as of yet, to unearth these sources.

[11] Sughra Mehdi, 'Mekhanon ka Pata (Safarnama Makkah, Madinah, Iraq, Iran, Sham)' in *Mekhanon ka Pata* (*Safarnama)* (Bhopal:

Earlier in the twentieth century, other Muslim women from South Asia also visited other parts of the Islamic world and wrote about their journeys, though not necessarily in the form of a pilgrimage narrative, like Sughra Mehdi. One of the earliest examples again appears to come from the Bhopal royal court in the form of a revealing chapter on Turkey and Egypt in Maimoona Sultan's *Siyasat-i-Sultani*, published first in Urdu and then in English translation as *A Trip to Europe*.[12] As these titles suggest, this account was actually written about Nawab Sultan Jahan Begum's journey to Britain in 1911, ostensibly to attend the coronation of King George V and Queen Mary, by her young daughter-in-law, just eleven or twelve years old at the time. Reflecting her esteemed mother-in-law's incremental approach to Muslim women's reform, Maimoona Sultan was extremely critical of the 'freedom' being sought by Turkish women, arguing that their slavish imitation of western culture was leading to an abandonment of religious injunctions.[13]

Madhya Pradesh Urdu Akademi, 2005), pp. 10-43. Also see her aunt Saliha Abid Husain's short piece on hajj in her travelogue, *Safar Zindagi ke liye Soj o Saj* (New Delhi: Maktabah Jamia Limited, 1982), p. 144ff.

[12] Maimoona Sultan, *Siyasat-i-Sultani* (Agra: Muhammad Qadir 'Ali Khan, n.d.); and *A Trip to Europe* (Bhopal: n.p., 1913).

[13] Maimoona Sultan, *Trip*, especially pp. 114, 126. On Sultan Jahan Begum's approach to Muslim women's reform, see my *Muslim Women, Reform and Princely Patronage: Nawab Sultan Jahan Begam of Bhopal* (London: Routledge, 2007).

Other West Asian countries also came under the attentive gaze of Indian Muslim women in the decades that followed. Sughra Humayon Mirza, editor of the Hyderabadi women's journal, *al-Nisa*, wrote an account of her trip to Iraq with her husband, a prosperous barrister, in the early 1920s, while Begum Hasrat Mohani, wife of the renowned journalist, poet and Khilafat politician, published not only a *Safarnama-i-Hijaz*, but also a *Safarnama-i-Iraq*, in the late 1930s—about which it was written that she displayed 'a keen observation and an eye for minute detail'.[14] As journeys to other parts of the Islamic world became more common for South Asian women in the post-independence period, so did accounts of their experiences in memoirs and journals. Consider, for instance, Masuma Begum's short piece on 'A Day in Samarkand' in a 1959 issue of *Roshni*, the journal of the All India Women's Conference;[15] Shaista Suhrawardy Ikramullah's concluding chapter in her *From Purdah to*

[14] The first of these books is listed along with other publications in the introduction to Sughra Humayon Mirza's later Indian travelogue, *Roznamchah Safar Bhopal* (Hyderabad: *al-Nisa* monthly, 1924), while the latter two are mentioned in a short biographical sketch of Begum Hasrat Mohani—entitled 'Hasrat's First Wife'—in K.H. Qadiri's biography of her husband, *Hasrat Mohani* (Delhi: Idarah-i Adabiyat-i Delli, 1985), p. 383—from which the quotation is also taken. Unfortunately, I have not, as yet, been able to locate any of the original texts.

[15] Masuma Begum, 'A Day in Samarkand', *Roshni*, September 1959, pp. 55-6.

Parliament on her 'years in Morocco' as Pakistan's ambassador in the mid-1960s;[16] and Abida Sultaan's brief reflections in her *Memoirs of a Rebel Princess* on her visits to Jordan to visit her ambassador son in the early 1980s.[17]

It is worth noting that most, if not all, of the women mentioned in the previous two paragraphs did not just write about journeys to North Africa and Islamic Asia, but also those to Britain and Europe as well. One case already mentioned explicitly was that of Maimoona Sultan, who, in *Siyasat-i-Sultani*, documented the experiences of her mother-in-law, herself and other relatives as they travelled—no doubt accompanied by an army of retainers—through Britain, France, Germany and, more briefly, other parts of Europe over many months in 1911. An underlying theme of this account was the limitations of travelling within purdah, made worse by the European's 'objectionable custom of photographing people of rank for cinematography shows and illustrated newspapers'.[18] Indeed, there are moments in the narrative when the reader wonders if the young girl saw much more than the inside of hotels or, at best, a

[16] Shaista Suhrawardy Ikramullah, *From Purdah to Parliament* (Karachi: Oxford University Press, 1998, rev edn.), ch. 24.

[17] Abida Sultaan, *Memoirs of a Rebel Princess* (Karachi: Oxford University Press, 2004), pp. 253-5.

[18] Maimoona Sultan, *Trip*, 49.

glance of a famous monument from the back seat of a curtained motor car.[19]

Nawab Sultan Jahan Begum's own account of this same journey, contained in two chapters of her autobiography as well as published speeches given at the ladies' club at Bhopal upon her return, and other reformist writings, offer proof that these experiences in Europe did not lessen her faith in the purdah system; on the contrary, they convinced her that the free intercourse of the sexes was a 'blot on the escutcheon of Western civilisation'.[20] Offering a rather more critical view, despite herself being an acquaintance of the Bhopali Begums, was Sughra Humayon Mirza in her *Safarnama-i-Yurop*, published in two volumes in 1926.[21] For her, the writing of a European travelogue was an opportunity to continue her campaign, as already set out in speeches at women's conferences, articles in

19 Ibid., esp. pp. 37, 49, 72.

20 Sultan Jahan Begum, *Al-Hijab or Why Purdah is Necessary* (Calcutta: Thacker, Spink and Co., 1922), p. 131. Also see Sultan Jahan Begum, *An Account of My Life*, vol. III, tr. C.H. Payne (Bombay: The Times Press, 1927), chapters XIV-XV; and 'English translation of a speech delivered by Her Highness the Nawab Begam of Bhopal, in the Ladies' Club, on 29 January, 1912' in *A Brief Decennial Report of "The Princess of Wales Ladies' Club," Bhopal* (Calcutta: Thacker, Spink and Co., 1922), p. 159. For further discussion, see my *Muslim Women*, ch. 4.

21 Sughra Humayon Mirza, *Safarnama-i-Yurop*, 2 vols (Hyderabad: 'Azim Press, 1926). My thanks to Gail Minault for sending me a copy of this text.

the Urdu press and books on her travels within India, against what she saw to be the Indian cultural practice of 'strict' purdah.[22]

In light of these differences of opinion, it is perhaps ironic that what appears to be the first published European travelogue by an Indian Muslim woman did not actually grapple with the purdah issue. This omission can be explained on the basis that its author, Atiya Fyzee—renowned in her own time as a writer, poetic muse and patron of the arts—was one of the first elite Muslim women in South Asia not to wear the veil. Indeed, she had been encouraged, as a niece of the celebrated Bombay-based reformer, Badruddin Tyabji, to play an active role in public affairs even before travelling to Britain in 1906-7 to take up a government scholarship at a teacher's training college. A distinctive feature of her narrative is its emphasis on the 'everyday': alongside her lively accounts of meeting local elites and prominent Indians abroad are detailed descriptions of clothes worn, meals enjoyed and domestic interiors. Perhaps reflecting her family's newly moneyed status, Atiya also paid particular attention to the activities of subaltern classes, thus providing a useful

[22] For evidence of all of these activities, see Sughra Humayon Mirza's *Roznamchah.* I have also discussed her particular arguments relating to purdah, as advanced at a women's conference in Bhopal in 1918, in 'Fostering Sisterhood: Muslim Women and the All India Ladies' Association', *Journal of Women's History,* 16:2 (summer, 2004), pp. 40-65.

documentary record for 'history from below'. In terms of style, what is significant about this account is that it appeared initially as serialised diary entries in the Urdu women's journal, *Tahzib un-Niswan*, before being published in book form under the title *Zamana-i-Tahsil* [A Time of Education] in 1922.[23]

This mode of writing—usually described in Urdu as a *roznamchah*—was also chosen by Atiya's sister, Nazli, the Begum of Janjira, when she wrote her own travel narrative upon visiting Europe in 1908 on an official tour with her princely husband,[24] as it was by Begum Inam Habibullah, wife of the taluqdar of Saidanpur in the United Provinces and, later, a Muslim League politician in her own right, when she travelled to Britain with her husband in 1924 to visit their three sons at boarding school.[25] Though it is not known what inspired the latter, it may be conjectured that the two

[23] Atiya Fyzee, *Zamana-i-Tahsil* (Aligarh: Matba' Mufid-i-'Am, 1922). For examples of her original contributions to *Tahzib un-Niswan*, see issues dated 26 January 1907-30 November 1907. An annotated translation of this text with comprehensive introduction will soon be published by Sunil Sharma and myself under the proposed title of *A Muslim Woman in Edwardian Britain: The Life and Travels of Atiya Fyzee Rahamin.*

[24] Nazli Rafia Sultan Nawab Begam Sahiba, *Sair-i-Yurop* (Lahore: Union Steam Press, n.d.). My thanks to Sunil Sharma for sending me a copy of this text.

[25] Begum Inam Habibullah, *Taziraat-i-Safarnama-i-Yurop* (n.p., n.d.). My thanks to the author's granddaughter, Muneeza Shamsie, for presenting me with a copy of this text.

Fyzee sisters' experiences of contributing to family diaries known as the *Akhbar ki Kitab*—kept by each branch of the Tyabji clan in their respective residences—may have encouraged them, first, to write about their travels and, second, to write in the way that they did. What is certain is that these unusual records books offer a rich source for accounts of Indian and foreign travel by men and women alike in that family members were especially encouraged to contribute upon arrival and departure.[26]

In light of this family tradition, it is perhaps not surprising that one of the earliest travelogues to the Americas by an Indian Muslim woman was also written by a member of the Tyabji clan, namely, Begum Shareefah Hamid Ali. When she was appointed India's representative to the Commission on the Status of Women of the newly founded United Nations in 1946, she decided, as former president of the All India Women's Conference, to write an account of her experiences for serialisation in the organisation's journal, *Roshni*. Unfortunately, she only got as far as describing her 'extraordinary' three day journey by air to New York, the first session of the Commission, her initial

[26] I consulted copies of the *Akhbar ki Kitab* from Matheran and Mahableshwar at the Nehru Memorial Library and Museum in New Delhi, but there are also copies from other branches of the family in the Bombay University Library and Arts Council, Aiwan-e-Riffat, in Karachi. A descendant of the family, Salima Tyabji, is currently doing research on the Delhi collections.

impressions of Washington D.C. and a visit to Mount Vernon before she was forced to return to India as a result of the 'serious situation'—assumedly connected with Partition as it was, by this time, mid-1947—in her hometown of Mussoorie.[27] Still, her brief epistles are remarkable for what they reveal about her own cultural confidence at this historic moment when India itself was about to carve out a distinctive position on the international stage in the form of non-alignment. Consider, for instance, the parallels that she draws between 'American-Indians' and 'negroes', as she calls them, and 'our ill-treated Harijans'—from which she concludes that, whereas segregation was 'passing' in India, it would remain a bitter reality for a long time to come in the United States.[28]

Depicting 'Amreeka' rather more favourably within the changing international circumstances of the Cold War, were a number of Bangladeshi women writing in the Bengali women's magazine, *Begum*, after it established a travel column in the 1980s. Mumtaz Wadud, for instance, described New York as a 'fairy's land', while Rafia Khan marvelled at technical innovations—digital clocks, flashing news headlines,

27 Begum Shareefah Hamid Ali, 'My Journey to America by Air', *Roshni*, 2:6 (July 1947), pp. 23-8; 'My Visit to America. II', *Roshni*, 2:7 (August 1947), pp. 16-22; 'Washington Diary III', *Roshni*, 2:8 (October 1947), pp. 23-6; and 'Excursion to Mount Vernon', *Roshni*, 2:9 (November 1947), pp. 5-7.

28 Begum Hamid Ali, 'Excursion to Mount Vernon', p. 7.

wall-sized televisions—on the streets of the same city.[29] The United States' growing status in the minds of Bangladeshi women is also suggested in articles published in the same context about travel to Europe, and Britain in particular, that were far less flattering. Salima Rahman, to take just one example, highlighed in her account that, rather than the streets being paved with gold, 'England is really made of earth' [*Bilet deshta matir*].[30]

Notably, there were also a number of American travel accounts written in the post-colonial era by Muslim women associated with academia. From Bangladesh, to continue this geographical focus, there was Sonia Amin's *Boston Diary Theke* [From the Boston Diary], written for a Dhaka newspaper, *Dainik Sangbad*, when the now professor of history at Dhaka University was studying in Boston in the 1980s.[31] Her short pieces

[29] Mumtaz Wadud, 'New York-er Bazaar' [Shops in New York], *Begum*, vol. 34, no. 27, 4 April 1982, p. 11; Rafia Khan, 'Shadure Ja Dekhlam' [What I saw far away], *Begum*, vol. 34, no. 38, 20 June 1982, p. 7. Also see Nilufer Khanam's serialised account, 'America Smriti' [Memory of America], *Begum*, starting in vol. 34, no. 44, 15 August 1982, p. 10. My thanks to Asha Islam for providing on-the-spot translation from Bengali when consulting these sources at Bangla Akademi in Dhaka.

[30] First in this serialised account is Salima Rahman, 'Bilet Deshta Matir' [England is really made of earth] , *Begum*, vol. 34, no. 39, 27 June 1982, p. 16.

[31] The author herself told me about this publication when I visited her in Dhaka in January 2006, but, unfortunately, was unable to locate a copy.

may be compared with those of the aforementioned Sughra Mehdi, former professor of Urdu at Jamia Millia Islamia in Delhi, who, in tribute to the fourteenth century Moroccan traveller, styled herself as 'Ibn Battuti' when recounting her journey to Britain, Canada and the United States in 1983.[32] A more well-known example from Pakistan is Sara Suleri's literary memoir, *Meatless Days*, in which she makes reference to her journey from 'her father's Pakistan' to the lecture halls of Yale where she is now professor of English.[33]

Other memoirs written by Muslim women from South Asia, too, describe their individual experiences of travelling, living and working in North America in the post-war period. Descriptions of travel by South Asian Muslims to Central and South America, on the other hand, remain few and far between—one extraordinary example being Abida Sultaan's account in her memoirs of her year as Pakistani ambassador to Brazil in the 1950s.[34] In terms of rarity of described location, it is matched only by *Aa Jao Afriqa* [Come Back Africa], written by the revered Pakistani feminist poet, Kishwar Naheed, upon her return from a women's conference in Africa in the 1980s—though its

[32] Sughra Mehdi, 'Mushahadat-i-Ibn Battuti' [Observations of Ibn Battuti] in her *Sair Kar Dunya ki Ghafil... (Safarnama)* (New Delhi: Nayi Awaz, 1994), pp. 47-87.

[33] Sara Suleri, *Meatless Days* (Chicago: University of Chicago Press, 1989).

[34] Abida Sultaan, *Memoirs*, pp. 223-5.

inclusion here may be questioned on the basis that she states explicitly on the text's first page that it is not a *safarnama* (travelogue) or an *aap biitii* (autobiography), but a *jag biitii* (world experience).[35]

Still, Kishwar Naheed's comment seems an appropriate one with which to lead into some preliminary conclusions as it suggests that, in looking at the way in which Muslim women in South Asia write about their journeys abroad, one ought not be fixed by the constraints of genre or tradition, but open to the overlap between various types of travelogue and other literary styles. Even in this brief survey, it has been seen how travel accounts appear in a whole variety of different forms—from book length *safarnama* and dedicated chapters in memoirs to serialised *roznamchah* and short pieces in journals and anthologies. Furthermore, the point has been made that sometimes these accounts draw on the long tradition of writing life stories and journeys in Islam, sometimes on a modern European model, and sometimes both—though there does appear to be at least a general progression in the modern period from a less reflexive style of writing, as symbolised by Sikandar's hajj account, to one that, like the writings of Sughra Mehdi, chart an inner, as well as a physical, journey. These sources, then, produced by a fascinating array of

35 Kishwar Naheed, *Aa Jao Afriqa* (Lahore: Sang-e-Meel, 1995).

Muslim women from across South Asia in English, Urdu and a variety of regional languages, provide a window into the lives of a group of individuals often twice-silenced as women and as Muslims. At the same time, they are illuminating as to a distinct type of history in which momentous public events, like the coronation of George V and the establishment of the United Nations, appear alongside 'everyday' happenings—the workings of the home, family relations, what people wear, what they eat. Thus, Muslim women's foreign travel writing offers a very particular insight, not only into the 'selves' of those who took time to write their journeys, but also the places they visited and the people they met in the Islamic world, Europe, the Americas and Africa: the cultural encounters that are at the heart of a world history that recognises the constitutive role of religion, gender and sexuality.

BIBLIOGRAPHY

I: Travel Writing by Muslim Women in South Asia

Ali, Begum Shareefah Hamid, 'Excursion to Mount Vernon', *Roshni*, 2:9 (November 1947), pp. 5-7.

——, 'My Journey to America by Air', *Roshni*, 2:6 (July 1947), pp. 23-8.

——, 'My Visit to America. II', *Roshni*, 2:7 (August 1947), pp. 16-22.

——, 'Washington Diary III', *Roshni*, 2:8 (October 1947), pp. 23-6.

Begum, Smt. Masuma, 'A Day in Samarkand', *Roshni*, September 1959, pp. 55-6.

Bhopal, Maimoona Sultan of, *A Trip to Europe* (Bhopal: n.p., 1913).

——, *Siyasat-i-Sultani* (Agra: Muhammad Qadir 'Ali Kharr, n.d.).

Bhopal, Sultan Jahan Begum of, *An Account of My Life*, vol. III, tr. C.H. Payne (Bombay: The Times Press, 1927), chapters XIV-XV.

——, *An Account of My Life*, vol. II, tr. Abdus Samad

Khan (Bombay: The Times Press, 1922), ch. XIV.

——, 'English translation of a speech delivered by Her Highness the Nawab Begum of Bhopal, in the Ladies' Club, on 29 January, 1912' in *A Brief Decennial Report of 'The Princess of Wales Ladies' Club,' Bhopal* (Calcutta: Thacker, Spink and Co., 1922).

——, *The Story of a Pilgrimage to Hijaz* (Calcutta: Thacker, Spink and Co., 1909).

Bhopal, Nawab Sikandar Begum of, *A Pilgrimage to Mecca*, tr. Mrs Willoughby-Osborne (London: Wm H. Allen & Co., 1870).

——, *A Pilgrimage to Mecca*, tr. Mrs Willoughby-Osborne (Calcutta: Thacker, Spink and Co., 1906).

Fyzee, Atiya, *Zamana-i-Tahsil* (Aligarh: Matba' Mufid-i-'Am, 1922).

Habibullah, Begum Inam, *Taziraat-i-Safarnama-i-Yurop* (n.p., n.d.).

Husain, Saliha Abid, *Safar Zindagi ke liye Soj o Saj* (New Delhi: Maktabah Jamia Limited, 1982).

Ikramullah, Shaista Suhrawardy, *From Purdah to Parliament* (Karachi: Oxford University Press, 1998, rev. ed.), ch. 24.

Janjira, Nazli Rafia Sultan Nawab Begum Sahiba of, *Sair-i-Yurop* (Lahore: Union Steam Press, n.d.).

Kakakhail, Professor Zainab Khatun, *Jalwah gah-i-tauhid ke rubaru: Safar-i-hajj aur astana-yi nabuwwat par haziri ki rudad* (Lahore: Himayatul-Islam Press, 1976).

Khan, Rafia, 'Shadure Ja Dekhlam', *Begum*, vol. 34, no. 38, 20 June 1982, p. 7.

Khanam, Nilufer, 'America Smriti', *Begum*, vol. 34, no. 44, 15 August 1982, p. 10.

Mehdi, Sughra, *Mekhanon ka Pata (Safarnama)* (Bhopal: Madhya Pradesh Urdu Akademi, 2005).

——, *Sair Kar Dunya ki Ghafil… (Safarnama)* (New Delhi: Nayi Awaz, 1994).

Mirza, Sughra Humayon, *Safarnama-i-Yurop*, 2 vols (Hyderabad: 'Azim Press, 1926).

——, *Roznamchah Safar Bhopal* (Hyderabad: *al-Nisa* monthly, 1924).

Mustafa, Saba, *Paharon ke daman men: Safarnama-yi arz-i-muqaddas* (Banglaore: Alaktrik Qaumi Pres, 1979).

Naheed, Kishwar, *Aa Jao Afriqa* (Lahore: Sang-e-Meel, 1995).

Rahman, Salima, 'Bilet Deshta Matir', *Begum*, vol. 34, no. 39, 27 June 1982, p. 16.

Rashid, Dr Sabrina Q., *Hajj: A Wonderful Experience: With a Guide to Hajj* (Dhaka: Islamic Foundation Bangladesh, 2005).

Suleri, Sara, *Meatless Days* (Chicago: University of Chicago Press, 1989).

Sultaan, Abida, *Memoirs of a Rebel Princess* (Karachi: Oxford University Press, 2004).

Wadud, Mumtaz, 'New York-er Bazaar', *Begum*, vol. 34, no. 27, 4 April 1982, p. 11.

II: Other Sources on Travel or Travel Writing

Ballantyne, Tony and Antoinette Burton, (eds.), *Bodies*

in Contact: Rethinking Colonial Encounters in World History (Durham: Duke University Press, 2005).

Birkett, Dea, *Off the Beaten Track: Three Centuries of Women Travellers* (London: National Portrait Gallery, 2004).

Burton, Antoinette, *At the Heart of the Empire: Indians and the Colonial Encounter in Late-Victorian Britain* (New Delhi: Munshiram Manoharlal, 1998).

Chatterjee, Kumkum, 'Discovering India: Travel, History and Identity in Late Nineteenth- and Early Twentieth-century India' in Daud Ali (ed.), *Invoking the Past: The Uses of History in South Asia* (New Delhi: Oxford University Press, 1999), pp. 192-227.

Dunn, Ross E., *The Adventures of Ibn Battuta: A Muslim Traveller of the 14th Century*, rev. ed. (Berkeley: University of California Press, 2005).

Eickelman, Dale F. and Piscatori, James (eds.), *Muslim Travellers: Pilgrimage, Migration, and the Religious Imagination* (London: Routledge, 1990).

Fisher, Michael H., *Counterflows to Colonialism: Indian Travellers and Settlers in Britain 1600-1857* (Delhi: Permanent Black, 2004).

Grewal, Inderpal, *Home and Harem: Nation, Gender, Empire, and the Cultures of Travel* (London: Leicester University Press, 1996).

Hasan, Mushirul (ed.), *Westward Bound: Travels of Mirza Abu Taleb* (Delhi: Oxford University Press, 2005).

Hrbek, Ivan, 'The Chronology of Ibn Battuta's Travels', *Archiv Orientalni*, 30 (1962), pp. 409-86.

Kosambi, Meera, 'Introduction: Returning the American Gaze: Situating Pandita Ramabai's American Encounter' in *Pandita Ramabai's American Encounter: The Peoples of the United States (1889)* (Bloomington: Indiana University Press, 2003), pp. 3-46.

Lambert-Hurley, Siobhan, 'Muslim Women Write Their Journeys Abroad: A Bibliographical Essay' in Shobhana Bhattacharji (ed.), *Travel Writing in India* (Delhi: Sahitya Akademi, forthcoming).

——, 'Pilgrimage—Islam' in *Encyclopedia of Sex and Gender* (Macmillan Reference USA, forthcoming).

——, 'A Princess's Pilgrimage: Nawab Sikandar Begum's Account of Hajj' in Tim Youngs (ed.), *Travel in the Nineteenth Century: Filling in the Blank Spaces* (London: Anthem, 2006), pp. 107-37.

——, 'Out of India: The Journeys of the Begum of Bhopal, 1901-1930,' *Women's Studies' International Forum*, 21:3 (June, 1998), pp. 263-76; reprinted in Tony Ballantyne and Antoinette Burton (eds.), *Bodies in Contact,* op. cit., pp. 293-309.

Lewis, Reina, *Women, Travel and the Ottoman Harem* (New Brunswick, New Jersey: Rutgers University Press, 2004).

Mackintosh-Smith, Tim (ed.), *The Travels of Ibn Battutah* (London: Picador, 2003).

McDonnell, Mary Byrne, 'Patterns of Muslim Pilgrimage from Malaysia, 1885–1985' in Dale F. Eickelman and James Piscatori (eds.), *Muslim Travellers,* op. cit., pp. 111-130.

Metcalf, Barbara D., 'What Happened in Mecca: Mumtaz Mufti's "Labbaik"' in Robert Folkenflik (ed.), *The Culture of Autobiography: Constructions of Self-Representation* (Stanford: Stanford University Press, 1993), pp. 149-67.

——, 'The Pilgrimage Remembered: South Asian Accounts of the Hajj' in Dale F. Eickelman and James Piscatori (eds.), *Muslim Travellers,* op. cit., pp. 85-107.

Morris, Mary and Larry, O'Connor, (eds.), *The Virago Book of Women Travellers* (London: Virago Press, 2004).

Pearson, Michael N., *Pilgrimage to Mecca: The Indian Experience 1500-1800* (Princeton: Markus Wiener Publishers, 1996).

Pratt, Mary Louise, *Imperial Eyes: Travel Writing and Transculturation* (New York: Routledge, 1992).

Robinson, Jane, (ed.), *Unsuitable for Ladies: An Anthology of Women Travellers* (Oxford: Oxford Paperbacks, 2001).

Said, Edward, *Orientalism: Western Concepts of the Orient* (New York: Pantheon, 1978).

Sen, Simonti, *Travels to Europe: Self and Other in Bengali Travel Narratives 1870-1910* (Hyderabad: Orient Longman, 2005).

Visram, Rozina, *Asians in Britain: 400 Years of History* (London: Pluto Press, 2002).

——, *Ayahs, Lascars and Princes* (London: Pluto Press, 1986).

Wolfe, Michael, (ed.), *One Thousand Roads to Mecca: Ten Centuries of Travelers Writing About the Muslim Pilgrimage* (New York: Grove Press, 1997).

IV: Other Quoted Material

Attewell, Guy, 'Authority, Knowledge and Practice in Unani Tibb in India, c. 1890-1930' (Unpublished PhD Thesis, University of London, 2004).

Baljon, J.M.S., *Religion and Thought of Shah Wali Allah Dihlawi 1703-1762*, (Leiden: Brill, 1986).

Berkes, Niyazi (trs. and ed.), *Turkish Nationalism and Western Civilization* (London: George Allen and Unwin, 1959).

Beveridge, Annette S., 'Introduction' to Gul-Badan Begum, *The History of Humâyûn (Humâyûn-nâmâ)*, third reprint (first published 1902), (Delhi: Low Price Publications, 1996).

Bhargava, K.D., *Descriptive List of Mutiny Papers in the National Archives of India, Bhopal* (New Delhi: National Archives of India, 1960).

Bhopal, Her Highness Nawab Shah Jahan of, *The Taj-ul Ikbal Tarikh Bhopal; or, The History of Bhopal*, tr. H.C. Barstow (Calcutta: Thacker, Spink and Co., 1876).

Bhopal, Sultan Jahan Begum of, *An Account of My Life*, tr. C.H. Payne (London: John Murray, 1910).

——, *Al-Hijab or Why Purdah is Necessary* (Calcutta: Thacker, Spink and Co., 1922).

——, *Hayat-i-Qudsi: Life of the Nawab Gauhar Begum alias The Nawab Begum Qudsia of Bhopal*, tr. W.S. Davis (London: Kegan Paul, Trench, Trubner & Co. Ltd, 1918).

Bose, Sugata and Ayesha, Jalal, *Modern South Asia: History, Culture, Political Economy* (London: Routledge, 1998).

Dale, Stephen F., *The Garden of the Eight Paradises: Bâbur and the Culture of Empire in Central Asia, Afghanistan and India (1483-1530)* (Leiden: Brill, 2004).

Eaton, Richard M., 'The Political and Religious Authority of the Shrine of Bâbâ Farîd' in *Essays on Islam and Indian History* (Delhi: Oxford University Press, 2000), pp. 203-24.

Fazl, Abul, *Akbar-nama*, vol. III, tr. H. Beveridge (Calcutta: Asiatic Society, 1939).

Hough, Major William, *A Brief History of the Bhopal Principality in Central India* (Calcutta: The Baptist Mission Press, 1845).

Khan, Shaharyar M., *The Begums of Bhopal: A Dynasty of Women Rulers in Raj India* (London: I.B. Tauris, 2000).

Lambert-Hurley, Siobhan, *Muslim Women, Reform and Princely Patronage: Nawab Sultan Jahan Begam of Bhopal* (London: Routledge, 2007).

——, 'Introduction: A Princess Revealed' in Abida Sultaan, *Memoirs of a Rebel Princess* (Karachi: Oxford University Press, 2004), pp. xiii-xxxix.

——, 'Fostering Sisterhood: Muslim Women and the All India Ladies' Association', *Journal of Women's*

History, 16:2 (Summer, 2004), pp. 40-65.

Lapidus, Ira, *A History of Islamic Societies*, 2nd ed., (Cambridge: Cambridge University Press, 2002).

Luard, C.E., *Bhopal State Gazetteer*, vol. III (Calcutta: Superintendent Government Printing India, 1908).

Malleson, Colonel G.B., *An Historical Sketch of the Native States of India in Subsidiary Alliance with the British Government* (London: Longmans, Green and Co., 1875).

Minault, Gail, *Secluded Scholars: Women's Education and Muslim Social Reform in Colonial India* (Delhi: Oxford University Press, 1998).

Mukhopadhyaya, Sambhu Chandra, *The Career of an Indian Princess: The Late Begum Secunder of Bhopal, K.S.I.* (Calcutta: Anglo-Sanskrit Press, 1869).

Powell, Avril A., 'Indian Muslim Modernists and the Issue of Slavery in Islam' in Indrani Chatterjee and Richard Eaton (eds.), *Slavery and South Asian History* (Bloom-ington: Indiana University Press, 2006).

Qadiri, K.H., *Hasrat Mohani* (Delhi: Idarah-i Adabiyat-i Delli, 1985).

Robinson, Francis, 'Religious Change and the Self in Muslim South Asia' in *Islam and Muslim History in South Asia* (New Delhi: Oxford University Press, 2000), pp. 105-121.

von Grunebaum, Gustave E., *Medieval Islam*, 2nd ed. (Chicago: University of Chicago Press, 1952).

——, *Muhammadan Festivals* (New York: Henry Schuman, 1951).